Research Writing Made Easy

RESEARCH WRITING MADE EASY

How to Snap the Pieces Together Correctly
And Efficiently, and Finish on Time

Richard P. Walters, Ph.D.
Stan E. DeKoven, Ph.D.

Vision Publishing ✦ Ramona, California

Research Writing Made Easy
How to Snap the Pieces Together Correctly
And Efficiently, and Finish on Time

This book is a revision and expansion of *Research Writing Made Easy: A Guide to Writing College Papers, The Masters Thesis, The Doctoral Dissertation and the Doctoral Project.* Copyright 2002 by Steve Deckard and Stan DeKoven.

Portions of this book appear in the same or similar form in *From Questions to Answers: Principles and Methods of Quantitative Research.* Copyright 2008 by Richard P. Walters and used by permission.

For information on ordering please contact:
Vision Publishing
1115 D Street, Ramona, CA 92065
760-789-4700
www.visionpublishingservices.com
Printed in the United States of America

Table of Contents

Foreword

Writing a college research paper, a graduate level thesis or dissertation, or doing a doctoral project can be a frightening prospect! The purpose of this book is to take the fear and frustration out of the process so that you complete the task with success and a smile on your face.

We respect what you have achieved thus far in your academic career and we are excited about what lies ahead for you. That's why we want to help you.

Between us, we've written more than fifty books plus many training programs, articles, and research reports. We've supervised and evaluated hundreds and research projects—undergraduate through doctoral. Each of these projects required the same processes of planning, gathering information, organization, and expression into words in order to convey facts, persuade, and motivate other people.

We will pass on what we have learned: the systems, the rules, and *especially the shortcuts*! We have tried to keep the explanations brief and clear. The technical aspects of form and style follow the *Publications Manual of the American Psychological Association* (5th ed.).

The faculty of Vision International University join us in hope and prayer that your studies lead you into ever more meaningful relationship with, and effective service to, our gracious God. We are with you in His family.

Rich Walters, Ph.D.
Dean, Pastoral Care and Counseling
Vision International University

Stan DeKoven, Ph.D.
President
Vision International University

CHAPTER ONE

Getting Ready to Write

Research papers and projects are big, but that does not mean that they must be difficult. If you have heard horror stories from people who were terribly frustrated by a research assignment, their problem was probably not the assignment itself but the result of not knowing how to do it one simple step at a time. *Research writing can be made easy.*

You've done the right thing—you got this book! It will show you how to plan and organize the project so you move steadily forward with confidence and finish on schedule with proper pride in the final product.

We won't kid you though. A substantial undergraduate research paper has many pieces and graduate research has many more. The good news is that you already know how to do most of the "pieces." It's organizing the whole series of events that can seem intimidating and be frustrating.

A jigsaw puzzle is assembled one piece at a time, a building is constructed one brick at a time, an elephant is eaten one bite at a time, and a research paper is written one sentence at a time. In each case it is a series of easy steps.

One puzzle piece is a pretty simple thing when you analyze it; hardly anything is simpler than a brick; a tasty forkful of elephant—well, we don't know. We know that a sentence is a pretty simple thing and that is the building block of writing. So, we'll help you brush up on writing skills and then we'll show you how to put it all together. Let's begin!

The Research Paper and Its Purpose

A research paper is a presentation of facts and opinions that are:
• Limited to a relatively narrow phase of a subject
• Original in selection, evaluation, expression, and conclusion.
• Based on facts gathered by: (1) reading books and articles written by people who are knowledgeable in a particular field, (2) using data compiled by organizations (e.g., census data), (3) interviewing

experts, or (4) collecting new data through systematic empirical methods.

• Presented according to a standard method or procedure.

Writing a research paper is carried out for a number of reasons and purposes. The need to write a paper may occur in the pursuit of one's own ministry or as a part of a task for a course. Perhaps the best reason is to satisfy one's own curiosity about something. (Hold on to that thought; it will come in handy as you zero in on the topic for your research.)

Whatever your purpose might be, you will need several items: (1) a clearly defined topic, (2) information, and (3) a process. This chapter describes how to define a topic (draw a picture of the building you want to construct) and get the information you will need (find the bricks). The rest of the book is about how to write it ("Bricklaying 101"), including adding a flag to the top of the building so everyone can look up and salute it. But first, a quick look at different types of research papers.

Different Levels of Complexity

Research comes in differing degrees of difficulty. One way in which the level of thinking in a paper is assessed is by a system known as Bloom's Taxonomy (1956). A *taxonomy* is a system of classification, in this case, of the complexity of mental processes.

Each level of the taxonomy requires a higher level of mental processing than the previous level. The lower end of the taxonomy is more concrete; the higher end more abstract, and therefore requires more mental capacity and effort to do justice to its goals. For example, it is easy to sort a group of cat and dog pictures into a pile of cat pictures and a pile of dog pictures. That is knowledge. It would not be easy to write a persuasive essay that encompasses all the reasons why dogs are better pets than cats. (Or vice versa.) Here are the levels of Bloom's Taxonomy as they may apply to portions of a research paper:

1. Knowledge: This is the portion of the paper that contains quotes and the facts, which are gathered in the research process.
2. Comprehension: This portion of the paper shows that the author has grasped the basic concepts from the literature reviewed in the research process.

3. Application: In this portion of the paper the author uses knowledge gathered from a variety of sources and applies it to his/her particular topic (subject) in a new and insightful manner.
4. Analysis: This portion of the paper shows an in-depth examination and breakdown of the facts and quotes and opinions.
5. Synthesis: This portion of the paper acts as "formation of the whole." It brings major elements together into a concise statement(s). This is where the primary thesis of the paper is developed.
6. Evaluation: This portion is where the writer makes personal statements and judgments about the value or purpose of the ideas presented in the paper.

Further information about the taxonomy is readily accessed on the Internet. Go to www.bloomstaxonomy.org or do a Google search, which will turn up many concise articles and guides.

Undergraduate Research

Undergraduate research papers usually are a summary of what others have already said or written on a given subject, with student observations and a critical analysis of the subject. Such a paper (often called a term paper) will normally present information that is already known, rather than contributing anything new to existing knowledge.

However, do not suppose that a research paper is simply an assembling of known data. Rather, the way that information is gathered from different sources can result in opening new interpretations of old ideas, with an opportunity for students to summarize, apply, analyze, synthesize, and evaluate. An undergraduate-level research paper can in fact contribute considerable information to the Christian community. The student should make a conscious effort to use all of the levels described by Bloom's taxonomy.

And, the student should always write from a biblical perspective. One's biblical perspective can be expressed in all of Bloom's levels. For example, one can relate a scripture to the material in a new and insightful way (application) or associate two passages so that each makes the meaning of the other more forceful than it was before (synthesis).

Graduate Level

Graduate level research papers should show evidence of all the elements of Bloom's Taxonomy, with particular use of the higher levels of thinking. Theses and dissertations are expected to show an original contribution to a field of study. This calls for great depth of understanding of the subject matter—gaining knowledge and comprehension—Bloom's two lowest levels, but without that preliminary work there can be no subsequent analysis, synthesis, and evaluation.

Different Types of Research

While there is a multitude of research methods, they can be put into two major categories: qualitative and quantitative. Neither is inherently superior to the other, but each fits certain types of objectives. Both involve elements of research design that are not within the scope of this book on writing.

Qualitative Research

The steps of qualitative research can be compared to making a quilt. Just as a quilter may search through many bolts of fabric and take a few squares from each of many different sources, a qualitative researcher may go through many books, journals, interviews, and archives to find relevant bits of information that are needed to create unifying and clarifying explanations and arguments about a theme. And, just like a quilt, the finished research owes a great debt to those who wove the cloth from which the final product is created, and which can still be identified in it. Qualitative research is inductive; it moves from the general to the specific.

Quantitative Research

Quantitative (empirical) research gathers and uses information that did not exist before the project began. It, too, begins with decisions about design and purpose, but it does not depend upon pre-existing material. It can be compared to weaving a blanket, starting by shearing a sheep to make into yarn to weave into the final product! It is deductive; it moves from the specific—a hypothesis—to the general. Quantitative research involves many steps that qualitative research does not require.

Neither of these methods is easier than the other; they are just different. Reports of qualitative research are generally far longer in word count because quantitative research uses numeric data and the language of statistics to represent opinions and abstractions in compressed form. It is a matter of choosing the approach that best fits the skills, temperament, and purposes of the researcher.

Getting a Topic

Picking the topic for a research paper is one of the most important tasks in the process. The topic needs to be rather narrow in scope. It is common to try to cover more than can be managed. Don't select, for example, "A History of Sin" as your topic! Follow your interests, especially when planning a lengthy graduate level endeavor. Do not grab a nearby topic just to complete the requirement. Find something that you are curious about and that will be useful to you.

It is helpful to anticipate whether all of the needed resources will be available: (1) access to published information (greatly aided by the Internet), (2) availability of participants for research, (3) adequate time, and (4) funding for printing, mailing, photocopying, or travel.

Hints for Selecting A Problem (Getting Ideas)

• Read articles with which you strongly disagree
• Problems often arise out of everyday experiences
• Read summaries and implications for further research at the end of research reports or dissertations

Some Questions to Ask About the Problem

• Is the problem interesting?
• Is it current?
• Will it add to existing knowledge? (Why write it if someone else has already written it?)
• Is it feasible? Is it within the realms of possibility to find enough material to justify study?

Gathering Information

Tips for Getting Good Information

Start by seeking information from scholarly journals. New information gets into journals sooner than into books. You will benefit immensely by access to academic-quality materials available in online databases. These are in databases sold by subscription to libraries, so check with your local community or university library. Electronic access, coupled with the concise style of journal writing, will help you get reliable information on your topic quickly.

Finding Information on the Internet

The site, www.worldcat.org allows you to search the catalogs of more than 10,000 libraries worldwide (more than a billion books). It will then identify the libraries with the book you seek, listing them by distance from your location. It is usually possible to get books through inter-library loan once you know where the book is. Talk with your local librarian about inter-library loan services.

ProQuest is one of the best databases of scholarly journals. For topics with a theological component, search the ATLA Religion Database, from the American Theological Library Association and available online.

For general Internet searches, Google Advanced Search is excellent. When searching the Internet try submitting a very specific request first. Try several phrases in Google's "with the exact phrase" option. If this works, you have the gold nuggets and diamonds in your hands right away; if not, broaden out. This is usually quicker than the reverse strategy. Use the thesaurus on your word processor to find alternate words. Since most fields of work and study use special jargon you may have a long dry spell until you hit the right words, but when you do it is likely to rain good stuff on you until you're drenched.

Find books by subject search at the U.S. Library of Congress: www.loc.gov. After identifying a book, you may be able to borrow a copy from another library through inter-library loan. (The Library of Congress does not lend.)

A subject search at major booksellers (www.amazon.com, or Barnes and Noble: www.bn.com) can locate the latest releases, and you may find books you wish to purchase. Look at their used books and comparison shop.

An easily searched website, www.tren.com, offers more than ten thousand Doctor of Ministry dissertations that are not found in Dissertation Abstracts or elsewhere, and hundreds of scholarly papers read at conferences. The nominal charge is a bargain if you find material that addresses your topic. There are many online archives of classic theological works. See Appendix B, "Additional Sources of Help."

You must be highly selective in what sources you cite in your paper, especially from the Internet. Tons of garbage is floating on the vast ocean of the Internet. You should not use any Internet material unless you can cite the URL and date of access, so keep track as you go. You are strongly advised to not use Internet material except that from government (.gov) or university (.edu) websites, or from databases of scholarly journals.

When you find an article that is right on target, search again by the author's name. E-mail your compliments and thanks to the author, then ask if they have published other articles on the same or a similar topic. You are likely to get help. Most university websites are easily searched for addresses and some post publications that can be downloaded from their site.

Use Only Authoritative Sources

Outcomes are no better than their inputs—garbage in, garbage out. Your research will be judged by the confidence its readers have in your sources of information.

Do not cite Wikipedia (www.wikipedia.org) as a source. It may be useful as a place to begin a new search, to "prime the pump," but at this time it is not regarded as authoritative because it has no oversight that can guarantee the quality of material posted there. Some of it is excellent; some of it (evidence shows) has been fabricated and seriously inaccurate.

It is to your advantage to use material from only the most reliable, prestigious sources. If readers don't believe the sources you quote they may not take seriously your recommendations or trust your original research. Don't cheapen your hard work by using sources that will be viewed as unreliable or intellectually lightweight by your readers.

The two tables on the next page summarize guidelines for acceptable use of Internet materials and periodicals in scholarly research. Review these and follow them, so that your work meets high standards.

16

Guidelines for Use of Websites in Research
Sources That Are Suitable to Use
✦ Information from an *independent* medical or other scientific enterprise of certifiable objectivity.
✦ A governmental agency. Either site, www.firstgov.gov or www.info.gov, is a good place to start. The Centers for Disease Control (www.cdc.gov) and Census Bureau (www.census.gov) have huge reservoirs of statistical data.
✦ A school or university
Sources That Are Inadvisable to Use
✦ Information from a commercial organization.
✦ An individual, except one with an incontrovertible reputation as a scholarly authority on the topic.
✦ An agency or organization that may be biased. E.g., The National Institute of Pork Rinds says that arterial blockage is good for you.
Information That Might Be Possible to Use
✦ When the information you use runs contrary to the expected bias of the website. For example, evidence about the health risks of smoking from a tobacco company's website.
The One Situation In Which Everything Is Eligible to Be Used
✦ Anything goes *only* if the Internet itself is the subject of the research.

The Use of Periodicals in the Review of Literature

Genre	Explanation and Role in Your Study
Academic Journals	*Academic journals* report scholarly endeavors—research studies, essays, theoretical reasoning—that have been reviewed by experts ("refereed") before publication. Most deal with a fairly narrow slice of a field of study, use the specialized vocabulary of that field, and may require some background knowledge of a field to be fully understood. They typically have only limited amounts of advertising, pictures are rare, numerical data are prominent. The writing style is precise and formal, fitting their purpose of concisely extending factual information and informed opinion. Access at graduate school libraries or electronic databases.
Trade Journals	*Trade journals* usually look like popular magazines but are geared to the interests of a particular industry. Articles tend to address practical "where the rubber meets the road" concerns of the industry. Neither systematic research nor theory are common, however, you may find statistical information or data about trends or regulations in the industry, or find leads to more detailed information. Bias is more likely than in scholarly journals.
Magazines for Specialized Audiences	*Magazines for intellectuals* (for want of a better term) often carry articles as detailed and authoritative as typical journal articles. Here, too, limited use that supplements scholarly journals may be acceptable in your research study.
Magazines for the General Audience, Newspapers	The purpose of *general circulation magazines* may be to inform, but entertainment is of at least equal importance. Elements such as flashy graphics, illustrations, slick paper, color printing, casual writing style, and lots of ads identify the genre. Not used at the graduate level unless popular culture or a news event is itself the subject of the study.
Always work with the full text; never rely on just an abstract or secondary report.	

Reference or Bibliography Cards

It is essential to keep a separate, complete and accurate record of each source of information consulted. An excellent method is to record the information onto a card as soon as a new source is consulted. Copy the information exactly as it appears on the title page of the book or article, using the same punctuation and abbreviations. Then you will have all the information needed for developing a reference list and constructing a proper in-text citation.

VIU follows the APA style for format, style, and references as defined in the *Publication Manual of the American Psychological Association* (5th ed). It is available at most local libraries or it may be purchased from *VIU*. The rules most commonly used are explained later in this book.

These cards can be sorted into alphabetical order when you are ready to type them into the computer.

Examples (Underlined words will be in italics in printed report)

For a book by one author

Author/Editor. Year.
Title/Edition.
Publisher.
Pages consulted.

DeKoven, S. (1998) _Grief Relief_ (3rd ed.). Ramona, CA: Vision Publishing. (pp. 44-46).

Give page numbers unless the entire book is used.

For a book by two or more authors

Authors.
Year.
Title.
Publisher.

Walters, R. & DeKoven, S. (2008). _Research Writing Made Easy_. Ramona CA: Vision Publishing.

For a periodical

Authors.
Year. Title.
Journal/Volume Number/Pages.

Harvey, V.S., & Carlson, J. F. (2003). Ethical and Professional Issues With Computer-Related Technology. _School Psychology Review,_ 32, 92-104.

Taking Notes

The most practical way to write a research paper is to use notes constructed from the various sources. If these notes are prepared properly, organizing the paper will not be difficult. Make notes in such a way that the source would not have to be consulted again. Notes should summarize in your own words the information obtained and adequate identification of the sources. If the source contains information that you intend to quote verbatim, the material must be copied *exactly*, including the original punctuation. Great care should be taken to avoid misrepresentation by lifting material out of context or by twisting the interpretation to suit your personal bias.

Helpful Suggestions for Taking Notes

Write notes on 4" x 6" cards. Some students prefer the smaller 3" x 5" index cards; but rather than needing several cards for the same reference, it is better to have all your information on one or two cards. It is advisable to write on one side of the card only. Be sure to indicate on the bottom of the front of the card if there is additional information on the back.

Have only *one reference* and *one topic or idea* on each card. The reason for this will be made clear later. Include on each card:
• The name of one specific topic.
• Identification of the source at the top of the card (author's name, title, and anything else needed for a positive identification).
 • Record in the left margin the pages where the material was found.
• Takes notes in your own words as briefly as possible, except when an exact quote is being copied. Incomplete sentences and abbreviations are permitted as long as you are sure the notes will be easily understood later when the paper is being written. *You must take care not to "read into" or summarize material from reference sources in a biased way.*
• Material that is quoted exactly must be enclosed in quotation marks. The proper use of quotation marks is discussed later.
• Record only facts new to you, or stated in a different way.
• For numerous sources it may be best to adopt a system where each source is assigned a number and each additional card for the same source is given a letter. For example, the third card for source number four would be marked 4C in the upper right hand corner.

Note-Taking Example

In this example, a reference card records the essential data for giving reference credit and building the reference list. The other card records data in enough to (a) help you remember it when it is time to write and (b) to guide you back to the original source to refresh your thinking and to ensure that you are using that

> Author/Year   Chant, K. (1994)
> Title *Strong Reasons: An Apologetic of the Christian Faith*
> Publisher Ramona, CA: Vision Publ.

> Ontological Argument
> Chant, "Strong"
> 151. Arg comes in 2 forms:
> 1. Idea of perfection requires pfctn. We wish for it because
> a. reality
> b. values
> 154. 2. Idea of God requires God
> Anselm (11th c): "God is that than which nothing greater can be conceived."

material accurately. These cards are also useful in organizing the sequence of your writing. Notice that the source information and the subject are easily located at the top of the card. Repeat the heading, source, and page number(s) on each data card. If you do not, it is likely that you will be digging through pages of material to find a missing item.

Plagiarism and Fair Use

Research, like all progress, builds upon the work of others. One of the early tasks in your research is to read what other people have done and have learned as they have made inquiry into the topic that now interests you. You will summarize, synthesize, and evaluate some of their work. Be glad that others have gone into your area of interest before you. Use what you learn from them. Give them credit for their good work. Document their contribution to your work with parenthetical citations in the body of your report and in the References section of the report. These procedures are explained in this book.

Plagiarism—presenting the work of another person as one's own—is a serious ethical offense. The plagiarist is both a thief and a liar, motivated by intellectual incapacity (can't do the work) or sloth (too lazy to do the work, perhaps even too lazy to try). The same charges prevail against a person who invents data, or who changes or rearranges data that have been collected.

How to Use This Book the Best Way

Although most of this book contains suggestions directed specifically to the writing of the masters thesis and the doctoral dissertation, undergraduates will find considerable help, especially in Chapters 5, 6, and 7. The information in this book is not intended to be comprehensive, for the purpose of the text is to make research writing *easy*. Only the most important general principles of grammar, format, and style are presented. Students who are committed to excellence (as Christians are, in all that they are and do) should obtain a copy of the *APA Publications Manual* (5th ed.) if they plan to do a considerable amount of writing, especially for publication. The APA manual is available at most college bookstores; used copies are available online. Material presented to *VIU* should follow the general rules set out in these pages.

We encourage you to develop the ability to write clearly. The skill will be useful to you in nearly everything you do, and the process of learning to write clearly is actually the process of learning to *think* clearly, and who doesn't want to do that?

References

American Psychological Association. (2001). *Publication Manual of the American Psychological Association* (5th). Washington, D.C.: Americal Psychological Association.

Bloom, B. S., Englehart, N. D., Furst, E. J., Hill, W. H., & Krathwohl, D. R. (1956). *Taxonomy of Educational Objectives:* Handbook I. Cognitive domain. New York: Mckay.

CHAPTER TWO
Write an "A" Undergraduate Paper

After choosing the topic and doing the literature research (this is where note cards are prepared), you are ready to write. The first step is to prepare an outline from the note cards.

To prepare the outline, sort the note cards into piles according to their headings. Put the cards containing facts on the same topic or idea (or some part of a topic or idea) together. Next, prepare the outline from the headings on the note cards. Arrange the cards in the same order as the outline. Then, write the first draft of the paper with the following things in mind:

- Material should be put into your own words (except direct quotes).
- Quotations should be used to emphasize important points or in support of your conclusions.
- Write in a formal and objective style. First person personal pronouns (*me, my, I, mine, we, us, our, ours*) are not used in this style of writing.
- For most undergraduate level papers you should reserve judgments or opinions until the last part of the paper, which may be titled, "Author's Reactions." The undergraduate level paper should never resemble an informal essay unless that is the assignment.
- The pages should be numbered.
- After you have edited the first draft, it is advisable to ask a friend or a fellow student to read the draft and make suggestions.
- Then re-read, critique, and revise carefully.
- The final draft is to be typewritten or word-processed, double-spaced with 1" margins all around.
- Use only one side of the paper.
- Provide a title page with an appropriate report title, your name, and course title and number.
- Submissions by e-mail should conform to the instructor's standards for file type and file name.
- If a print copy is submitted, follow instructions given for the course. Fancy, decorated covers are not used.

• Always make a copy for your own files. As a rule, papers will not be returned to the student unless major corrections need to be made.

Write in clear and concise English with correct usage of grammar and spelling. When using a computer, use the spell-checker. The step of proofreading and checking spelling is a very important part of the process of writing, but be aware that the spell-checker will not catch every type of error. Have a friend who spells well and understands grammar proofread it for you. Reviewing your paper against the "Checklist for Manuscript Submission" (APA, 2001, pp. 379-383) can help assure that your paper conforms fully to professional standards.

Preparation of the References

A research paper is incomplete without a listing of all references consulted and used in the preparation of the paper. The reference cards are used to supply the required data. The format for constructing a reference list is described fully in Chapter 4 of *Publication Manual of the APA* (2001), pages 215-281.

The APA style manual (2001) refers to the bibliographic part of a paper as "References." Call the citations "References" and place them at the end of the paper. Do not use footnotes as a substitute for the References section.

If the reference cards are constructed properly from the beginning, you will have little trouble assembling a reference list. The references are an alphabetical arrangement of all the sources (including books, articles, films, interviews) used in preparing the document. The reference list should only contain items which have been cited in the text of the paper.

Should you wish to compile a list for further reading or additional sources not used in the actual preparation of the paper, these should be compiled in a list separate from the References and labeled "Additional Readings."

Suggested Procedure

• Arrange the reference cards alphabetically according to the author's last name. If no author is indicated, alphabetize the entry by the first important word of the title. If the reference is published by a society and no author's name is given, consider the society as the author.

• From the reference cards thus arranged, make a list that will appear at the end of the paper. Word process the reference list from your alphabetized note cards. For further help on the specific order of the reference list, consult 4.04 on pages 219-222 of the *Publication Manual of the APA* (2001).

• Punctuate as shown in the examples on the following pages. When the entire source has been consulted for a background of information, page numbers need not be included.

• Include only those references actually used. If a publication source referred to is from another source, the source that the information is from should be cited, not the source in which you found it.

The Completed Paper

The completed paper should indicate the student's mastery of the subject matter, research methods, and mechanics of language.

1. The title page should include
   a. Title of the paper
   b. Writer's name
   c. Date submitted
   d. Course number and title
2. The table of contents should show
   a. A list of the main divisions of the paper
   b. The page number on which the treatment of each main topic begins
3. The pages of the text should be
   a. Typed on one side of the paper only
   b. Single-spaced
   c. Documented with in-text citations
   d. Clearly numbered (the first page of text being page 1)
   e. Word processed, typed and printed with a clear image to facilitate grading
4. The references should list only the books and articles used in the final writing of the paper. Other sources may be listed in the section entitled, "Additional References."
5. If an outline of the paper is required, it should be submitted in approved form. See the sample outline provided in Chapter Four.

Self-Evaluation Checklist

Now that you have completed your research paper, you may wish to check your work by answering the following questions. The answers will indicate strengths and weakness and whether or not you have written a successful paper.

Subject Matter

- Did you limit your subject sufficiently?
- Have you sought out original, significant, varied source material?

Reference Cards

- Did you record all bibliographical information as you used each reference source?
- Have you copied the information exactly as it appears on the title page of your source, using the same punctuation and abbreviations?

Note-Taking

- Did you take notes in your own words, in phrases rather than in sentences, using lists and modified outline form?
- Did you copy direct quotations exactly, enclose them in quotation marks, and record the specific page on which the quotation was found?
- As you progressed, did you organize your material according to major divisions and sub-points?
- Do all your note cards have specific topic headings, and does the material on the cards refer directly to the topic or idea heading?

Writing the Paper

- Were you able to arrange your note cards according to your plan of organization with the help of the headings on the cards?
- Did you discard those notes that did not directly pertain to the limited subject upon which you decided?
- Have you utilized direct quotations sparingly, to embellish an idea, or to strengthen your point?
- Did you create effective, meaningful, original sentences from the notes you took?
- Is the style of your paper lively, original, interesting, and at the same time serious, objective, scientific, and accurate?

• Have you interpreted your notes objectively, avoiding misleading conclusions by taking material out of context?
• Did you have someone else read your paper critically?
• Did you spell check your paper?
• Did you make full use of your computer tools?

Footnotes and Bibliographic References

• Have you acknowledged all ideas that were not original with you and are not generally or widely known?
• Have you strictly observed the correct citation and reference style?

References

• Were you readily able to arrange your references at the end of the paper according to the proper form, directly from the information recorded on the reference cards?
• Did you list only the references you have actually used and cited in the text, omitting those sources that may have been referred to in the source material consulted?

Title

• Is the title of your paper original, brief, and meaningful?

Title Page

• Did you complete a title page according to the model provided?

CHAPTER THREE

Write an "A" Thesis or Doctoral Proposal

Prior to doing the actual thesis or dissertation you will be required to submit a proposal that describes clearly and in detail what will be done, how, and why it is a worthy project. Doing this gives you an opportunity to think through the entire research process and elicit feedback from your mentor and other advisors. Do not regard this as a chore or as a task that has to be done for others; keep in mind that *you* are the one who benefits. And benefit you will, because the process will help you create research with valid and useful results.

Broadly speaking, research can be of two types. Their methods are different, so the proposals for the two types are a bit different.

The Proposal for Qualitative Research

The first type is typically classified as qualitative and does not have a standard format or set of categories. It does, however, need to be structured and organized to ensure logical investigation and clear communication. Should you desire to do this type of thesis, the following basic outline should be followed:

1. A statement of what you propose and expect to do
2. A statement about the participants and/or artifacts to be examined
3. A statement about the methodology and the data collection
4. A discussion regarding possible ethical issues

Before doing this type of thesis or dissertation the student should consult with the staff at *VIU*.

The Proposal for Quantitative Research

The second type is known as quantitative. The following outline is to be used in preparation of a quantitative proposal.

1. Introduction
   a. Statement of the Problem
   b. Review of the Literature
   c. Statement of the Hypothesis (Or if more than one, "hypotheses")
2. Methodology
   a. Subjects

      b. Instruments
      c. Procedures
   3. Analysis of the Data
      a. Data Organization
      b. Statistical Procedures
   4. Significance of the Study
      a. Implications
      b. Applications
   5. Time Schedule and Budget
      a. Time Schedule
      b. Budget
   6. References

This proposal is a part of the grade for *Introduction to Research I*. This is a required class for all students who are writing a thesis or a dissertation. Recall that it is very valuable for the student to write a thesis if they plan to do doctoral work. The student should work with the *VIU* staff on the production of the proposal. The proposal will serve as the guide for writing the thesis or dissertation.

Most of the proposal is written in future tense. You will change it to past tense when the research has been completed (it is not difficult to do that), but it is much easier to think and write in future tense while you are planning.

The proposal is your plan. The better the plan, the fewer surprises or detours when you carry out the plan. Plan carefully—that's the *easy* way!

The proposal is an incomplete version of what will become Chapters 1, 2, and 3 of your final report. When you read Chapter 4 of this book you will understand how the proposal transforms into part of the final report.

Guide to Content Of A Proposal

This is meant to be a guide only and may have sections which are not necessary for your particular proposal. A proposal has three chapters.

Chapter 1: Introduction

The first chapter is usually the shortest but it is strategic by providing an overview of the project. It contains no personal pronouns (e.g., I, me, our) or value statements (e.g., should, needs) and it only sparingly includes findings from the research and theories of authoritative writers (which will be given generous attention in Chapter 2). The first chapter introduces

• What the author intends to study
• Where the information is to be found
• How it fits into a historical and social context.
• What is expected to be discovered
• And it may define words or terms that are used in the study that are unique to the field of study or have a different meaning than usual.

The topics, terminology, and sequence of topics used in proposals for and reports of major research projects are somewhat standardized. This book follows the commonly accepted usages. Each chapter should be organized into logical sections and subsections, depending on your topic and the length of the chapter. A suggested outline for each chapter is provided in this book, as exemplified below. Adapt these as your project requires.

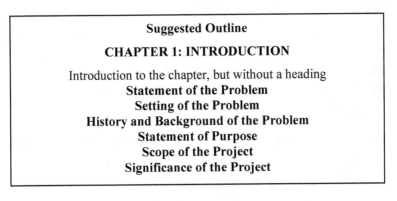

Suggested Outline

CHAPTER 1: INTRODUCTION

Introduction to the chapter, but without a heading
Statement of the Problem
Setting of the Problem
History and Background of the Problem
Statement of Purpose
Scope of the Project
Significance of the Project

Paragraph of Introduction to a Chapter

Each chapter should begin with a brief paragraph that describes the purpose of that chapter. These paragraphs do not have a heading. The purpose of the introductory paragraph to a chapter is like a TV promo—a quick preview of what is to come. Except for Chapter 1, two or three sentences will probably be enough. The example below illustrates how an introduction can prepare the reader to understand what comes next.

Worship is an attitude displayed toward God as we come before him both privately and corporately. Methods and styles of worship are varied and individuals tend to develop strong emotional allegiance to the practices they prefer. Worship style is one of the most common ingredients fueling conflict within churches in our culture today. Although Christians should know that God is more concerned with the content of our heart than our methods, worship wars flourish and church families are being torn apart. The focus of this study was to examine the preference of worship style of members and regular attendees at Meadowview Community Church.

This chapter sets out the thesis statement for the research, defines its objectives, describes the historical and social contexts in which the research took place, and identifies the potential significance of the project. Subsequent chapters review research done elsewhere on closely related topics, describe the methodology and findings of this research, and discuss possible application of the findings for Meadowview in particular and implications for other congregations.

Note that the author has introduced what lies ahead and provided an overview of the material that will be covered. Although this introductory section is from a dissertation, the principles that apply to writing an introduction for shorter projects are the same.

Statement of the Problem

This is a concise statement of the *what* of the study. You will also write a purpose statement, which will be the *why* of the study.

• The problem statement describes the problem as it exists today.
• The writer must make sure that the statement of the problem is neither too vague nor too broad in scope.
• The statement of the problem can be expressed in the form of a question or as a declarative statement, a choice that is left to the writer.
• The limits of the problem should be clearly stated. This is necessary to eliminate factors that will not be considered in the study.
• Terms that are unlikely to be familiar to the reader should be defined the first time they appear.
• A problem statement may easily be crafted by beginning with "The problem is . . ." and then describing the issues that remain problematic.

Some common errors in writing a problem statement are:

• Selecting a research topic too soon. It is essential to read and review as much of the existing literature as possible to assure that the you do not select a topic (problem) that has already been researched and extensively reported. The doctoral student must present a project that is innovative or creative and related to some aspect of ministry.

• Selecting a topic that is too broad in scope. Here the student must learn the skill of delimiting the topic. Delimiting is a term that means to "limit" the topic to parameters that are reasonable for a dissertation.

Examples
1. The issue of contemporary worship in comparison with traditional worship seems to evoke conflict in many churches.
2. The problem to be examined is the effect that excessively difficult leisure time activities have upon persons with dementia.
3. The problem is that many persons diagnosed with diabetes forego opportunities to learn how to manage their disease.

History and Background of the Problem

In this section the writer sets the problem into its historical and social context. It is a discussion of past problems, their origin, conditions that may have led up to the present problem or situation, and a survey of the consequences of the problem under investigation (e.g., who is affected, costs, secondary problems resulting from the primary problem). This review in Chapter 1 is at the level of a summary. Sources are cited, but much more detail is provided in Chapter 2. The section reveals where further research needs to be conducted and helps orient the reader to what the present study will examine.

Statement of Purpose

In the Statement of Purpose (sometimes called a "thesis statement") the author spells out what he/she hopes to accomplish by the project. It emphasizes the *why* of the study over the *what* that was described by the Statement of the Problem.

The section can begin with "It is the purpose of this study to . . ." One or two sentences will be enough. Specifically, this section will present a novel way to deal with the problem or "barrier" discussed above. Use words such as *describe* or *discover* for qualitative studies and *determine* or *investigate* for quantitative studies.

Nature and Scope of the Study

This is a very important part of the proposal. It is here that the author suggests what the limits or parameters of the study will be. Often a doctoral committee will suggest to the student that the study proposed is too broad or not broad enough for a dissertation or a project. It is better to discover this fact before embarking on a long project that will be overwhelming or simply fall short of the requirements of the university.

Under this heading the author suggests, in abbreviated fashion, how the study is to be done. All of this is given in detail in Chapter 3.

Significance of the Study

In this section, the author justifies the study by suggesting how the findings will be of use to the researcher, to other researchers, and perhaps even to the discipline in general. For example, a study of attitudes toward various translations of the Bible that compares attitudes held within one congregation toward the KJV, the New KJV, and the New Living Bible could help minimize dissension within that congregation but, combined with data from many congregations, could also contribute to understanding attitudes held collectively by conservative believers.

Chapter 2: Review of the Literature

Typical Outline

CHAPTER 2: REVIEW OF LITERATURE
Brief paragraph of introduction to the chapter without a heading.
Sources Consulted
Other Level Two Headings
Level Three Headings As Needed
These headings are created as appropriate to
the material in the chapter.

In the proposal the writer should present a thorough review of the literature that pertains to the topic under study. This foundation of information should be thorough and complete. According to Ary

(2005), the review of literature should (a) include only literature relevant to the proposed study, (b) does not have to be exhaustive, (c) should exhibit the author's firm grasp of the field of study, (d) should include theories and research results contrary to the stated hypothesis, and (e) should conclude with a discussion of the findings and their implications.

The review must be cohesive and illustrate how the studies are related to the statement of the problem. It is to be organized by topic, not just presented as a disconnected series of abstracts.

Where and How to Gather Relevant Literature

You can do most of the literature search from your computer. See Appendix B about Internet sources. But also get into the best community or university library near you. There are several places within a library to find references to materials that contain information pertinent to your research:

- The card catalog, which nowadays is on a computer
- The *Index to Periodic Literature*
- Professional journals
- Encyclopedias
- Means of identifying the experts in a particular field of study
- Internet searching in subscription databases the library has that you could not otherwise access
- Larger libraries have a staff member—a "Reference Librarian"—who specializes in helping visitors find information. The professionals will have ideas about finding material that will be useful to you. Just ask!

You will do well to become aware of the resources of the public and college libraries in the form of computer research capabilities. Most resources are usually available only in the larger libraries. Many of the main public libraries have what is referred to as "Computer Search." Almost any topic imaginable can be researched through this program. The student may need to get some assistance from the librarian. Librarians are noted for their willingness to help; do not be reluctant to ask.

After researching as many sources as possible and organizing the note cards into sections, you are ready to begin constructing an outline of the chapter. The outline is very important as it will ensure cohesion

34

(a smooth logical flow of ideas) and avoid disjointed writing that is difficult for readers to follow.

From the outline, you are now able to construct paragraphs that will present the reader with a well-organized flow of the material that was found in the research. Chapter 2 is devoted to a review of what other writers had to say about the topic. Refrain from expressing your own opinions or commenting on the ideas and concepts in this chapter. Your findings are reserved for Chapter 4 and your opinions for Chapter 5.

The purpose of the literature review is to provide the historical background for the study, a basis for its theoretical framework, and current research developments. It provides an interpretative summary of the topic. A good review critiques the research studies and shows how the findings relate to the problem being studied. This chapter provides the link between existing knowledge and the problem being studied. The purpose may be used to focus the reading and literature search. Present or past tense is used in writing this chapter. Differentiate between literature and research. There should be smooth transitions into sections and from one paragraph to another.

Early in the process of constructing and writing a review of literature search for what we call a "Bullseye Article." This is a recent (last year or two) journal article (usually research in nature) which zeroes in on the main idea(s) that are considered in your study's problem statement. Such an article will most likely contain many references that can serve as the base for much of the review. Finding such an article will save you considerable time while focusing the literature search on relevant and fruitful articles and books.

Another tip for the early part of the literature search is to find a dissertation or thesis (similar to a "Bullseye Article.") on the topic being studied. This serves as a goldmine of information and sources. Dissertations are referenced in *Dissertation Abstracts International.* You can find this at most college libraries. The most recent two years accessed on the Web at http://wwwlib.umi.com/dissertations.

Introduction

The introduction to Chapter 2 has no heading. It provides a reorientation to the purpose of the study and refers to the topics to be covered in the chapter.

Sources Consulted

Directly after the paragraph of introduction to the chapter insert a Level 2 heading for a section, Sources Consulted. Generally one paragraph is sufficient. It is simply a list of the places you went (actually or virtually) to find information: Include how the review was conducted, the search engines utilized, libraries visited, authoritative persons interviewed, and "key words" used to locate material.

Topical Presentation of Information

The order of topics can be arranged in a deductive manner (general to the specific). Discuss the existing knowledge base and identify the gaps in knowledge and make a link to your study. Also include a review of research studies that have contributed to current understanding and contribute to the need for your study. Use subheadings as appropriate to the content.

Summary

Provide a brief summary of the literature reviewed and be sure to link to the methodology of your project. Discuss the existing scientific knowledge base for your problem and identify gaps in the knowledge base, while making reference or linking to your study and methodology.

Chapter 3: Research Design

This is a "meaty" and detailed chapter because the entire design of the study is laid out. You will describe the research design, methodology, population, sample, and research methods, that will be used to examine the problem that was presented in Chapter 1. This should be done with enough detail that another person could do what you did and get the same result.

Chapter 3 is, essentially, a set of instructions about how to do the research. The good news is that once you have worked it out in step-by-step sequence you will know exactly what you are doing throughout the remainder of the research. You will benefit immensely from the effort required to develop an excellent Chapter 3.

The chapter begins, as each chapter does, with an introduction without a heading that gives the reader direction for the content covered in the chapter. Generally a one-paragraph introduction is sufficient.

The chapter might start, "The purpose of Chapter 3 is to present the (quantitative or qualitative) design and procedures that will be used to answer the research questions presented in Chapter 1: (repeat the question.)" Then proceed systematically to describe the research design methodology that will be used in the study, with an explanation as to why the particular methodology was chosen.

Outline

CHAPTER 3: RESEARCH DESIGN
Paragraph of introduction to the chapter
Problem Statement
Hypotheses
Hypothesis 1
Hypothesis 2
Operational Definitions
Assumptions
Limitations
Procedures for Gathering Data
Population
Sample
Instrument(s)
Data Collection
Time Schedule
Procedures for Analyzing Data
Organization of the Data
Test of Hypothesis 1
Test of Hypothesis 2

Problem Statement

This is simply repeated from Chapter 1. It is for the convenience of and clarification for those who do not read the full report.

Hypotheses

A hypothesis is a concise statement of the anticipated results written in a form that can be tested by objective methods. In the past many schools insisted on this being expressed in a negative or "null" fashion called the "Null Hypothesis." In some disciplines this is still used but *Vision International University* elects to have hypotheses expressed in a positive form.

A hypothesis is a provisional statement—an educated guess or hunch—that will either be rejected or accepted as a result of the research. In quantitative research, a hypothesis sets up a comparison that can be tested by gathering and organizing data that can be converted into numbers that will show or not show support for that hypothesis. For example:

> Men will report more frustration when having to wait more than one hour at a doctor's appointment than will women, as measured by the XYZ Frustration Survey.

A hypothesis is not usable without its operational definitions, given in the next section.

Operational Definitions

"Dictionary definitions" (also called "nominal definitions") answer the question, *What is it?* Nominal definitions are descriptive. "Operational definitions" answer the question, *"How do you find out how much there is of it?"* Operational definitions lead to an action—to doing something—thus their name.

To carry out our "doctor's office project" we need information on gender and frustration from a group of people. We will gather that using the XYZ Frustration Survey. The Operational Definitions are:

> Frustration: The score on the XYZ Frustration Survey (XYZFS).

> Gender: The response to item 1 on the XYZFS.

The operational definition tells the reader where the information used to test the hypothesis was obtained.

Now, just to show you how easy a research design can be, let's finish that project. Let's suppose you get a hundred people to complete the XYZFS. All you need to do is to sort them into two piles, men and women. You score each one. On the XYZFS, the higher the score, the more frustration. You calculate the average score for the group of women, and the average for the group of men. Which is higher? If the men score higher as a group than the women scored as a group, the hypothesis is supported. Now that wasn't difficult, was it? It took some time, but it wasn't hard.

Assumptions

Assumptions are listed for both quantitative and qualitative research. Identify any things that may influence the project. For example: that the participants understood the survey questions and answered them honestly, that the instrument used to measure the construct under study did in fact measure that construct and was not measuring something else, and that the people in the sample represented the population from which they were selected.

Limitations

Limitations are weaknesses that impact the results of the study. They are factors that are outside the researcher's control; "natural conditions that restrict the scope of a study and may affect its outcome" (Charles, 1998, p. 366). Research can rarely control all of the conditions that may influence its results, even in laboratory settings, and control can never be complete in field studies done in the social sciences. Compromises must be made for research to be done. Then reduce the "goodness" of the data that are collected. Examples include: a sample of small size, the fact that self reports are not fully reliable, or a sample that is not randomly selected.

Delimitations

Delimitations (not to be confused with limitation) are limits to the generalizability of the study. These are under the control of the researcher, and allow you to narrow the scope to a specific population or set of artifacts. In other words this would include those factors that impose on the breadth and depth of the study. As an example we look at Grant (2002).

The subjects for the study were a sample of Kansas high school science teachers obtained under the following headings: advanced biology, advanced chemistry, advanced physics, anatomy and

physiology, applied biology, applied chemistry, astronomy, biology, chemistry, earth and space science, geology, life science, physical science, physics, principles of technology, and zoology from the KSBE web site at:
http://www.ksde.org/labels/tchr_labels.html

This means that the outcomes of the study do not apply to, for example, (a) elementary science teachers in Kansas, (b) high school science teachers in Nebraska, or (c) teachers of English, social studies, and wood shop. In other words, the study is *delimited* by Grant's definition quoted above. His study focused on what the high school teachers reported they believe and teach about the topics surveyed. It examined relationships among the variables but did seek to specify causal relationships.

Don't Be Reluctant to Identify Limitations and Delimitations

Research writing is more credible when its integrity is clear. Please be candid and straightforward by completely describing all limitations and delimitations. Knowledgeable readers know that your research has limits; show that you know it too. Failing to point them out may result in your reader thinking that you are ignorant, a sloppy thinker, or trying to mislead them, none of which belongs in research done by Christians.

Procedures for Gathering Data

The last two sections of Chapter 3 are written in the style of an instruction manual, and there are good reasons for doing so. Two traditions of quality research are replication and peer review. Replication means that if another person carried out the same procedures they would, presumably, get the same results. Writing explicitly allows for that to happen. It also allows other persons to evaluation your methods, so that if your outcomes result from defective methods this will be noticed. The most compelling reasons for writing all procedures out in detail is that (1) it forces you to think through every part of your project before you do it, and (2) it allows your advisors to guide you into a plan that will provide accurate results. You can't get help working in secrecy. This section will have several components:

Population

The population is the total number of people (or artifacts) that might have been in the study. It is the larger group that is represented by the smaller group, the sample. The size of the population is always given. If people are being studied, describe the characteristics that are relevant to the study. For example: the distribution by age, gender, education, income, marital status, faith preference, race, and place of birth. You will know what these are for your own study.

Sample

These are the subjects (in our context, usually people) who have been selected for measurement. State the size of the sample and discuss how the size was determined. (Ideally, this is done by consulting a table that has been constructed by statistical analysis. Such a table is found in most research design texts.) Describe how the people (or artifacts) were selected from the population, including whether or not it was a random process. If it was, identify the type of random process. If it was not random, state that it was not in this section and also in the limitations section.

Instrument(s)

Here is described the means of gathering data. When you can, use a pre-existing instrument that has strong reliability, validity, and normative data. Include that information in this section. Describe the scoring method.

Put a copy of all measurement instruments in an appendix. Include letters of permission to use the instrument, if applicable.

If you develop a test or survey for the project, it should be tried out on people from the population, but who will not be in the sample. This is called a "pilot study," and the procedure usually reveals that some people will not understand parts of what you have prepared in quite the way you expected them to. This is valuable to know because you can then improve the instrument. The results of research cannot be better than the method of measurement. Discuss specific plans and statistics for testing the reliability and validity of your instrument if you are able to do that.

Data Collection

Provide a step-by-step description of the procedure, e.g., explain how subjects are assigned to groups (if applicable), what is done to whom, when, sources of data, and when and how data are collected. Provide a copy of the protocol and/or flow chart of the data collection process in an appendix. Describe procedures to standardize treatments and data collection. Place samples of data collection forms in an appendix and refer to them in this procedure section. Describe the plans for organizing, recording, and scoring data.

If a survey will be used, report the number that will be distributed. (Later you will report how many were returned.)

Time Schedule

This is a chronology of research process. It lists the major events during the time the work will be carried out. The Time Schedule may be presented as a list as shown in this example:

Submit final copy of proposal 10-24-07
Get letter of permission to gather data 11-1-07
Begin gathering data 11-8-07
Complete gathering data 11-22-07
Rewrite first three chapters 1-15-08
Tabulate data; enter into Excel 2-1-08
Analyze data 2-8-08
Finish Chapter 4 2-20-08
Finish Chapter 5 2-27-08
Assemble front and back matter 3-3-08
Send to instructor for critique 3-10-08
Revision and final printing 3-24-08
Oral presentation and submission 4-3-08

The greatest benefit of doing this is that it forces you to set target dates that will, if followed, ensure that you complete the project on schedule. When the project is completed, the dates set in the proposal are adjusted to the actual dates, if different.

Ethical Considerations

Discuss ethical considerations and the review process that should be followed. Discuss risk/benefit ratio and identify steps to minimize any risks. Place cover letter and/or consent forms in an appendix. Be sure to include in the appendix the forms and approval from the *Vision International University* staff.

Procedures for Analyzing Data

Again, you benefit by thorough advance planning. The more completely the procedures are described ahead of time, the easier it will be to do the work when you have the data.

Describe the plan for data analysis. (a) How the demographic data will be analyzed. (b) How each research question or hypothesis will be analyzed. (c) Identify the level of significance you would use. In the final thesis or dissertation this section is eliminated at this point and becomes a part of chapter 4.

Organization of the Data

Depict how the data will be recorded for tabulation, whether by hand or in a database program such as Excel. Include more information than seems to you to be necessary because it must be fully clear to a first-time reader.

Tests of Hypotheses

Explain, in sequence, the calculations that will be made that lead to a test of each hypothesis. If the steps are identical for each hypothesis, so state; if different, show all details for each.

CHAPTER FOUR

Write an "A" Thesis or Doctoral Report

The report is easier to write than the proposal, particularly if you have explained the procedures of data analysis well in Chapter 3. The process of writing the latter two chapters and finishing the report includes four components: (1) adapting the proposal to a report by changing from future to past tense and making adjustments as needed in Chapters 1 through 3, (2) writing Chapter 4, a somewhat bland process of reporting what happened, (3) writing Chapter 5, which is highly creative because it is evaluative and oriented toward application of the findings, and (4) adding front and back matter. Look forward to all of this.

Overview of Writing a Thesis or Dissertation

A thesis or dissertation for quantitative research will typically contain the following elements. They will appear in the sequence listed.
- Title Page
- Copyright Page
- Certification Page
- Abstract
- Dedication and/or Acknowledgement Pages (optional)
- Table of Contents
- List of Tables (if there are more than five in the document)
- List of Figures (illustrations, charts and graphs; if more than five)
- List of Abbreviations or List of Symbols (unlikely to be needed)
- Glossary (optional, and used only if the research requires many unfamiliar terms). It would be alphabetized, with hanging indentation, as used in this entry.
- Chapter 1: Introduction
- Chapter 2: Review of Literature
- Chapter 3: Research Design
- Chapter 4: Summary of Results
- Chapter 5: Conclusions and Recommendations
- References
- Endnotes (if used)
- Appendices
- Vita

Thesis and Dissertation Writing Details

The following sections give the reader a detailed description of the process for writing a thesis. These details are mostly for the "quantitative type" although they can be used to assist in writing a "qualitative type" of thesis or dissertation (see discussion in Chapter 1). Typically a thesis or dissertation is divided into five chapters. The discussion that follows uses such a format.

Front Matter in the Report

The pages before Chapter 1 are referred to as *front matter* and appear in the sequence listed earlier in this chapter. See Chapter 5 in this book for information about how to format the front matter.

The Title

A good title is important. Just as your entire project seeks to be an objective pursuit of facts, the title must be objective. When writing the title strive to be informative, not cute. For example, instead of the title *Only A Loser Will Keep Working for a Loser* you might use *The Relationship Between Supervisor Personality and Employee Turnover*. Keep the title short—no more than twelve words if possible—but use as many as needed to describe what your research accomplishes. Include words that will help other researchers identify the content of your report.

Both the thesis statement and the hypotheses summarize the research, so it is helpful to look at them as you create the title. You must choose words carefully, a process that may help you sharpen your thinking about the entire project. The title may not be a question nor may it include a subtitle.

The Abstract

The abstract appears at the front of the report, but it is written last. An abstract is a short unbiased summary (no more than 250 words) of the main elements of the research: introduction to the subject, description of what was done, results, and the meaning of it all. It incorporates the most essential information of chapters 3, 4, and 5 in extremely condensed form. It may be the most difficult part of the research report to write, because it must clearly describe many procedures and results in a few words.

With a limited budget of words, you must decide what is most likely to be of interest to your reader. If it were a sports story you'd tell what sport it was (procedure), who won (the result), and how it affected standings in the league (significance). Same thing here—procedure, result, significance. Make sure that the abstract is clear to someone who knows nothing about the topic of your research. It can be brief; just enough of an overview to show that it was a carefully executed empirical study. (A report of an NFL game doesn't recite the rule book.) Use what is in the thesis statement, although you may put it in other words. State each hypothesis and whether it was supported or not supported. Brag about the significance if you want to; you deserve to be excited about your good effort and it is acceptable to put some energy into your language even while it is formal.

Chapter 1: Introduction

The primary task is to change from future tense to past tense. Where it was correct to write in present tense in the proposal, no changes need to be made. Add new information and make adjustments of fact to conform to actual events.

Chapter 2: Review of Literature

It is always appropriate to add more relevant information. If you can organize the sequence of material so that the ideas develop more logically, do so. Evaluate if the contextual support links to your original work as well as it can, and strengthen those connections as much as you can.

Chapter 3: Research Design

It is common for procedures to change during the course of a project. Rewrite to record what actually occurred. No explanation is necessary, unless the change materially altered the outcome of the study.

Again, change from future to past tense as appropriate. Several sections need particular attention:

46

Assumptions and Limitations Sections

It is likely that you will identify more items to add to these sections during the course of the project. Be candid; disclosure helps build a strong report; silence may give the impression of ignorance.

Data Collection

Chapter 3 gives the plan for data collection. Results are reported in Chapter 4.

Time Schedule

Change target dates to actual dates.

Chapter 4: Summary of Results

An introductory paragraph without a heading starts this chapter. This is the chapter in which you report the data that have been gathered, describe their analysis, and summarize the findings. You will state if each hypothesis has or has not been supported by the data. In addition, you may include any findings that were not anticipated in the statement of the problem or purpose.

Data Collection

Report how many instruments were returned, and of those the number usable. If subjects were used, how many completed the entire project. Report any unusual occurrences or complications.

Data Presentation and Discussion

This is a presentation of the results of the analysis. State the first hypothesis in italics, then begin a new paragraph and report the data related to it. Data are first reported without commentary. This may lead to sentences that seem cumbersome and are uninteresting to write, but are factual and important. State whether each hypothesis was or was not supported (or confirmed). Do not use the word "prove!" For example:

Hypothesis 1 was tested by comparing the means of the sums of scores for the Fatigue Scale (items 5-9 of the survey. Males reported a mean of 17.8 and females a mean of 13.5, as shown in Figure 1. Hypothesis 1 was supported by the data.

In studies with several hypotheses, much of the writing will be structured identically for each of the hypotheses. Tables and figure are used as needed. See Chapter 6 in this book for specific instructions about placement of tables and figures.

Limitations and Assumptions (see these topics in Chapter 3)

At this time the assumptions and limitations should be reviewed. It is not unusual for circumstances to arise during the research process that require changing the original plan and these changes may impose or reveal some additional limitations. You may become aware of more assumptions that underlie the research. These should be incorporated into the report by revising the appropriate sections in Chapter 3.

Other Findings

Here you can include any additional patterns or unusual isolated findings that may be observed in the data even though they are not associated with any of the hypotheses. This section is sometimes called "Serendipitous Findings." Do not stretch to find something to build into such a section, but if you have something you think is worthy, include it.

Chapter 5: Conclusions and Recommendations

Start with an introductory paragraph without a heading. In this chapter you discuss what the results of your research mean. It is your opportunity to show the value of your work. Use your best thinking. The content should exhibit the higher levels of Bloom's taxonomy:

Analysis: contrast your work with that of others, deduce implications from your findings, relate the new information to old data and to current events, illustrate how it can be used.

Synthesis: combine your findings with those of others, devise ways to use your information, generalize (cautiously) to parallel situations, predict how the information can change something.

Evaluation: Assess and defend the significance of your work, convince the reader to take action in a particular way, judge the value of the potential outcomes from your recommendations.

Chapter 5 is not a time to be bashful or to hold back on your opinions. If you have been objective in gathering the data that lead to your conclusions you are entitled to be passionate in championing the use of those conclusions, however you may wish.

Naturally, you wish to be persuasive, so you will avoid shrill bombast and heavy-handed, dictatorial statements. Instead, you draw upon skills of thoughtful argumentation. Draw the total essence of the study together into a cohesive, integrated unit. Use authoritative material from the review of literature (Chapter 2) and the results (Chapter 4), and combine them in a way that wins the reader to your point of view.

Apart from the general objective in delivering the value of your effort into the hands of others, there is no one right outline for a final chapter. The following sections are typical.

Conclusions

Present the conclusions for the study. Summarize what has been learned.

Recommendations (or Implications)

Identify the how the new information can be used. Depending on the focus of the particular study, there may be sets of recommendations (or implications) for several different groups: for organizations, teachers, ministers, Christians, non-Christians.

Think broadly but sensibly. Do not try to turn a thimbleful of data into a "bathtubful" of recommendations—but if you have confidence in what you have done, get as much benefit from it as you can.

Implications for Further Research

Identify the implications for further research. State how the study could be done better if it were done again, or how it could be applied in a different population, or how it could be enhanced and elaborated upon.

A good research effort generates as many questions as it answers. It is not a bad thing at all if you still have unanswered questions when you are finished. We hope you do, and that your first research project whets your appetite for another—after you have rested from the first one!

References

Any reference cited in the narrative must appear in the reference list and be formatted according to APA Guidelines (5th ed.). References should include:
- Current material dated within the last ten years, though exceptions are necessary for foundation and background
- Foundation authors related to the issue/problem
- Authors with contrasting views
- More primary than secondary sources

Appendices (or Appendixes, if you prefer; either word is correct)

Long documents, lists, tables, graphs, and other supporting materials that would not fit smoothly in the flow of the text are included in appendices. The various entries are titled, have a heading formatted in the same way as a chapter heading but lettered instead of numbered, and are referred to in the main text where needed by use of parenthesis such as: (See Appendix C for details). Put appendices in the order in which they are cited in the narrative.

Examples of material that might be in the Appendix include:
- Copy of measurement instruments and data collection tools
- Tables, graphs, and other material not included in the narrative
- Consent forms
- Approved *VIU* forms
- Study budget and timetable

A Final Note

It is important to remember that this book is intended to be a brief set of guidelines. Not all of the questions of style and form are addressed. The student should be able to do a completely adequate job of writing his/her thesis or dissertation with this student guide. Any questions that are not answered in the guide can be referred to the *Vision* office and help will be provided where needed.

Although it should be the aim of every student to write with the very best style and to use the best English, grammar and syntax, the main purpose of the paper is to communicate important Christian principles. The student should never become so bound by the rules of writing that he/she loses the anointing and blessing of the Lord in their writing. It is never a waste of time to ask someone, particularly someone who may be aware of the various rules of grammar, to read the paper and make suggestions for improvement. Even professional writers have editors who read and critique their work.

The administrators and faculty at *Vision International University* want every student to know that we are much more interested in the actual content of the paper than in the mechanics of the writing. So, do the best you can and experience the joy of learning. Recall that the Bible states: Study to show thyself approved unto God and to do all things to the glory of the Lord.

Many helpful suggestions are in Appendix A, and Appendix B will lead you to information databases and tutorials. You are probably aware that websites may disappear, but more good ones continue to appear. And, use the tutorial and templates on the CD that came with this book.

Writing Right: Grammar, Punctuation, and Such

A short review of the important elements of written language should prove helpful. Much of the following information may seem elementary to most students, but it is offered as a review in the hope that some future problems will be avoided.

The English language includes two concepts that are easily confused: *parts of speech* and *parts of a sentence*. Each word in the English language is identified by a descriptive term. How that word is used in a sentence is described in a different way. The student must become familiar with these different terms in order to avoid becoming confused about the comments made by an editor or instructor.

The Parts Of Speech

The English language is made up of eight parts of speech, they are:
- Noun
- Pronoun
- Verb
- Adverb
- Adjective
- Preposition
- Conjunction
- Exclamation

There are times when some of these parts of speech will be used in a sentence in such a way that they become something else (mention will be made later of this confusing phenomenon). The following notes on each part of speech are elementary.

Nouns

A noun is the name of a person, place, thing, a state of being, or a quality. The name of a particular person, place, or thing (as in Jack, Mary, New York) is referred to as a *proper noun*, and is always capitalized.

Person	Jack, Mary, captain, man
Place	New York, home, store, jail
Thing	hammer, bat, ball, hangnail
State of Being	loneliness, dead, sick
Quality	love, patience, kindness

Pronouns

A pronoun is a word that takes the place of a noun and has the quality of person. As a rule of thumb, it is best not to write a term paper, thesis, or dissertation using the first person pronouns (unless they appear in a direct quotation).
- First person personal pronoun: I, me, my, mine, we, us, our, ours.
- Second person personal pronoun: you, your, yours.
- Third person personal pronouns: he, him, his, she, her, hers, they, them, their, theirs, it and its (for animals or organizations). Note that the pronoun is "its;" "it's" is the contraction of "it is."

Verbs

A verb is a word that shows a relationship or shows action.
- Relationship: "George is our captain." George and captain are the same person. Also called a connecting or intransitive verb.
- Action: "George hit the captain" George did something to the captain, who in this case is a different person. Also called a transitive verb.

Adverbs

An adverb is a word that modifies a verb, adjective, or other adverb.
- "George walked slowly to the door." *Slowly* tells how George walked.
- "George had a very large dog." *Very* modifies *large*, an adjective.
- "George walked very slowly to the door." *Very* modifies the adverb *slowly*.

Adjectives

An adjective is a word that modifies or describes a noun.
- "The immense elephant stormed the village." *Immense* is an adjective that modifies the noun *elephant*.

Prepositions

A preposition introduces a prepositional phrase.
- "A bushel of apples sold for over four dollars." *Of apples* is a prepositional phrase that modifies or describes the noun *bushel*.
Prepositional phrases sometimes cause writers problems. They mistake the *object* of the preposition for the *subject* of the sentence. For example, "The group of boys was lost for days in the forest." The

word *group* is a collective noun that is treated as a single item. It is easy to use the wrong verb in this sentence: "The group of boys were lost in the forest." In this instance the verb must agree with the subject of the sentence, *group*, and not with the object of the preposition, *boys*. More will be said about this common problem in the section that follows.

Conjunctions

A conjunction is a connecting word, for example, *and*.
- "Apples and oranges are very good for you."
- "George ran to the door, and Mary jumped through the window."
In this case, *and* is used to connect the two parts of a compound sentence.

Exclamations

Exclamations are words such as *Oh!* and *Ah!*, which are almost never used in formal writing.

The foregoing discussion of the parts of speech is very brief and not intended to cover all the ways the parts of speech are used. If you have problems in this area, it would pay to purchase a writing guide such as *The Little, Brown Essential Handbook for Writers* (Aaron, 2002) or refer to pages 40-61 of the *Publication Manual of the APA* (2001).

The Parts of a Sentence

This section deals with the use of the parts of speech in a sentence. As a word appears in a sentence it often takes on a different name. For example, a noun can be the subject of the sentence, the object of the verb, the object of a preposition, or a predicative nominative.

Subject

The subject of the sentence is the word or words that tell what the sentence is about. The subject is either a noun or a noun substitute.
- "George hit the ball." *George* is the subject of this sentence.
- "George and Mary walked to the store." *George and Mary* make up the compound subject of this sentence.

Predicate

> • "George hit the ball." *Hit the ball* is the complete predicate. *Hit* is the verb.

Direct Object

In the sentence just above, *ball* is the direct object of the verb.

Predicate Noun

> • "George is our captain." In this sentence *captain* is a predicate noun. This means that *captain* and *George* are the same person.

About Verbs

Because some of the rules about verbs are difficult, it is important to have a working knowledge about what these rules mean.

Action or Relationship

A verb is a word that shows action or a relationship between two nouns.

> • "George hit the ball." *Hit* is an action verb. Action verbs are also called transitive verbs.
> • "George is our captain." *Is* is a linking verb. These verbs are referred to as intransitive.

Verbs may show time or tense (past, present, or future). Other tenses of verbs include future perfect, and past perfect. Most of the more complicated tenses will not be a problem for the student writing a term paper, thesis, or dissertation. However, to be safe it is advisable to purchase an English textbook for reference purposes.

A Matter of Agreement

The most frequent problem that students and writers in general have with verbs has to do with agreement. The English language requires that the verb must agree with the subject.

> • "George is our captain." *George* is a simple subject, singular, and takes the verb *is*, a singular verb.
> • "George and Mary are our captains." *George and Mary* is a compound subject (plural), and takes the plural verb *are*.
> • "The lion is a fierce animal." In this sentence, *lion* is a singular noun, and it takes the singular verb *is*.

• "Lions are fierce animals." In this sentence, *Lions* is a plural noun, and it takes the plural form of the verb *are*. The point here is that the subject of the sentence and the predicate noun must agree in number.

Predicate Adjective

A predicate adjective is a word in the predicate part of the sentence (follows the verb) that describes the subject.

• "George is lazy." *George* is the subject. *Lazy* is the predicate adjective.

The Adjective as a Modifier

The adjective is a describing word (modifier) and can be used in many parts of a sentence. Most of the time adjectives modify or describe nouns. Adjectives answer the questions: What kind? Which one? How many?

• "The white house on the crooked street was painted by the old man." *White* describes the subject, *house,* a noun. *Crooked* describes *street,* a noun, the object of the preposition *on. Old* describes *man,* a noun, the object of the preposition *by*.

About Adverbs

The Adverb as Modifier

Adverbs modify by answering the questions: How? When? Where? Why? To what extent? The adverbs are underlined in the examples just below.

• How—The boy ran <u>quickly</u> to the store.
• When—The boy rested <u>after</u> he returned home.
• Where—The boy fell <u>down</u>.
• To what extent—My picture was the <u>most beautiful one</u> in the exhibit.

Adverbs also describe words. Adverbs describe (modify) verbs, adjectives, and other adverbs. For example, notice the part each word plays in this sentence:

The very large house burned very quickly.
The very (adjective) large (adjective) house (noun)
burned (verb) very (adverb) quickly (adverb).

In the sample sentence the words *The house burned* would be called the simple sentence. All the other words are modifiers.

Please note that it would have been incorrect to write, "The very large house burned quick." When a word that is usually an adjective, such as quick ("The quick boy ran the bases on a single") is used as an adverb (telling how the fire burned) it will almost always end in "ly." For example: quickly, softly, safely, badly.

About Pronouns

The use of pronouns can be tricky (see pages 47-50 of APA Manual). As noted before, a pronoun is a word that takes the place of a noun. Pronouns are classified in many different ways. Listed below are some of the more common classifications of pronouns. Only the pronouns that cause the most problems are listed here:
- First Person Singular Nominative = *I*
- First Person Singular Objective = *me*
- Second Person Singular Nominative = *you*. In formal writing, the use of this pronoun should usually be avoided, as should the use of *I* and *me*.
- Third Person Singular Nominative = *he, she, it*
- Third Person Singular Objective: *him, her, it*

Pronouns may also show possession: *his, hers, mine, my, its, their*. Of course there is also the infamous second person singular possessive pronoun, *your*. It is best left out of formal writing. Several problems with pronouns will be discussed later, but it is advisable to mention the most common errors at this time in the hope that repetition will help.
- Wrong: "Mary sent the letter to Bill and I. Me and Bill were late."
- Correct: "Mary sent the letter to Bill and me." (The pronoun *me* is the object of the preposition *to*, and as the object it must be in the objective case). "Bill and I were late." (The pronoun *I* is part of the compound subject and as a part of the subject it must use the nominative case.)
- Wrong: "Between you and I, it doesn't matter who wins."
- Correct: "Between you and me… " (*me* is part of the compound object of the preposition *between* and needs a pronoun in the objective case).
- Wrong: "You and me are the only ones left to clean up."

• Correct: "You and I are the only ones… "

About Prepositions

The following are prepositions, and they usually introduce a prepositional phrase: *to, in, from, into, with, on, over, under, of, at.*

"Bill and I went to the ball game." "*To the ball game*" is a prepositional phrase that answers the question "Where?" and is therefore also an adverbial phrase. In such phrases we say that *to* is the preposition and *game* is the object of the preposition. The object of a preposition is almost always a noun or a noun substitute.

Probably the most common error made with prepositions is to put the preposition at the end of the sentence.

• Not good: "We couldn't decide who to give the cake to."
• Better: "We couldn't decide to whom to give the cake." Here the preposition is together with its object. The above example may sound awkward, because it is not the way we usually speak, but it is grammatically correct and therefore the best usage in formal writing. This rule does not apply, of course, if you quote someone's actual words.

About Articles

The only words that have not been presented so far are the articles, which are words that serve one purpose only; articles point to a noun! The articles include: *the, a, an* (and some would include *this, that, these, those,* but never *them*). The main problem that a writer may have with articles is using *a* where *an* is correct.

Common Errors

There are certain grammatical and punctuation errors that are frequently made even by some of the best students. See pages 41-60 of the APA Manual to review them.

Commonly Confused Words

It may not be necessary for you to learn all the nuances of these words, but it *is* necessary that all language in your report is correctly used. You are encouraged to have at least one person who has strong command of correct grammar and word usage to read your paper before you finish.

There, they're, and their

58

- *There* is an adverb and answers the question "where?"
- *They're* is a pronoun-verb contraction meaning "They are."
- *Their* is a possessive pronoun (third person). "Their car was stolen."

Its and it's

- *Its* is a possessive pronoun. "The bird flapped its wings."
- *It's* means "it is." "It's later than you think." (Contractions are not used in formal writing).

To, too, and two

- *To* is a preposition. "We went to the country yesterday."
- *Too* is an adverb that usually means also or to what degree. "My brother wanted to go too, but was too late."
- *Two* stands for the number 2. "It was two o'clock."

Principal and principle

- *Principal* is a person. "John was the principal of the school." One helpful way to remember which is which is to remember that the principal is a real "pal."
- *Principle* means a fundamental rule or law, doctrine, or assumption. "The principle rule of love is caring."

Alot and a lot

- *Alot* is not a word. It should be "a lot."
- It would be better to find another word to use in the place of "a lot" (many, a large percentage of), and better still to find precise data.

Affect / Effect

These two words are frequently needed when writing about research in the social sciences, but they can be very confusing. Part of the confusion arises because each can be used as a noun and as an verb. These are the most common usages:

Affect (noun): Used often in psychology to mean feeling or emotion, as in "His affect was cheerful."

Affect (verb): To influence or change something; to produce an effect, as in "He wants to affect people."

Effect (noun): 1. A result produced by a cause; a consequence, as in "His speech had a great effect." 2. The power to produce a results; influence, as in "His style has a persuasive effect." *Effect* (verb): To bring about; to produce a change, as in "The speech had the results he liked to effect."

That / Who

That refers to objects or conditions; *who* refers to people. "The surveys that were returned by people who attended the concert were tabulated."

Cite / Sight / Site

Cite means to quote or document. "The author cited *The Journal of Fine Art* in her report."
Sight refers to vision. "The sight of the American flag stirs my patriotism."
Site is position or place. "Coolidge Park was built on a site formerly occupied by a factory."

Accept / Except

Accept is a verb, to agree or receive: "Mr. Magoo was proud to accept the award."
Except is a conjunction that denotes an exception: "All the men were members of the club except Burford," or a verb, to exclude or leave out: "He was excepted from membership in the club."

Words That Are Not Used in Formal Research Reporting

Etc.

Research writing is about clarity. Et cetera (along with "and so on," which is the English equivalent of the Latin) is vague. Be specific; that's the way it is done.

Approximately

The goal of research is to move from vagueness and imprecision to greater certainty and precision. Avoid this word, and similar words, that are inexact.

I, me, mine

Research writing is about objectivity, which calls for leaving ourselves out of the picture. Yes, the writing becomes a bit more stilted, but that's the way it is done. If it is in a quote, leave it.

Prove

Science does not even claim to be able to prove the sun will rise in the east tomorrow morning. We think it likely, but science cannot prove it. Show data and probabilities, but, unfortunately, you cannot prove anything.

Always, Never

Don't use words such as these that indicate absolutes—unless, of course, you can *prove* that there is *never* an exception. Omit these words. Always! Never use them!

Agreement of Verb and Subject

Were and was

"The excited group of boys (*were, was*) playing in the street." In this sentence the verb should be "was playing" because the verb must agree with the subject "group" which is singular. "Boys" is the object of the preposition.

Is and are

"One of the trees (*is, are*) out of place." "Is" agrees with the subject (noun), "one."

Correcting Style Errors

Passive Voice

The passive voice in a sentence can usually be found by the use of the form of the verb "to be" followed by a past participle (see page 42 of APA Manual). For example, "A good time was had by all." A better reading would be: "Everyone had a good time." Too many passive voice sentences will make a paper difficult and boring to read. Added examples:

   • Passive Voice: "The results of the study were not considered by the committee."

• Active Voice: "The committee did not consider the results of the study."

Long Sentences

One of the first rules of good writing is brevity. The writer should always endeavor to avoid long, complicated sentences that are not only difficult to read, but often miss the point completely. Long sentences are not necessarily the sign of a good writer.

Incomplete Sentences

A complete sentence must have a subject and a predicate, linked by a verb. Incomplete sentences (often called a sentence fragment or simply "frag") are not acceptable in formal writing. An editor will often write frag to indicate an incomplete sentence.

The following example is not acceptable: "The entire class under the leadership of the pastor and the elder board with full approval of the district superintendent." It is an incomplete sentence. It needs a verb.

Participial Phrase

A participial phrase at the beginning of a sentence must refer to the grammatical subject. "Running swiftly through the forest, John saw a boy accompanied by two dogs." In this sentence the running refers to John. If the writer wants it to refer to the boy, he must change the sentence to, "John saw the boy, accompanied by two dogs, running through the woods."

A participial phrase should not begin with a preposition:

• Wrong: "On arriving in San Diego, John's friends met him at the airport."

• Correct: "On arriving in San Diego, John was met by his friends at the airport."

A Final Word About the Quality of Good Writing

Written language, like any form of language, has one purpose. That purpose is to communicate ideas, information, and/or feelings. Writing may be classified as General, Business, Technical, Fiction, Informal, Formal, or Custom.

The rules for general, informal and fiction are more relaxed than for formal writing. Custom writing has to do with a special style designed by the author for a special purpose. Some poetry and prose intended to evoke feeling is written in creative ways for that purpose. This textbook deals only with the more formal style of writing, such as may be found in the technical or business style. The information in this book should be considered as the minimum standard expected of college level writing. Some students may need to refer to a refresher course in English, such as Barron's *English the Easy Way*.

A number of years ago, this writer came across a research paper that has long since been misplaced, making it impossible at this time to give proper reference to the author. Over the years I have taught the simple, yet profound findings of that piece of research. The essential points are included here.

The researchers sent questionnaires to over twenty-five of the most successful authors living at that time. An overwhelming majority of the authors questioned agreed that good writing has three qualities: brevity, clarity, and cohesion. The serious student would do well to read the following discussion of these qualities and endeavor to incorporate them into his or her writing.

Brevity

Generally speaking, the longer a sentence is the more difficult it will be to understand. The readability of writing is judged by two things: (1) the length of the sentence, and (2) the difficulty of the words used. Please accept the sad reality that most readers are impatient and are unlikely to look up a word they do not know or to linger to figure out unclear writing.

The general rule about brevity is "Never use twenty words to say something that could just as easily be said in eight to ten words." A writer must not sacrifice meaning in order to be brief, but every effort should be made to keep sentences and paragraphs as short and to the point as possible. Most English professors will agree that long sentences are often awkward and will often contain errors in grammar (such as dangling participles and incomplete clauses). For assistance in developing a concise writing style see pages 24-26 of the Aaron's book, *The Little, Brown Essential Handbook for Writers* (2002).

Clarity

Although brevity is a quality of good writing, it is never to be a goal in writing at the expense of clarity. In order to communicate well, writers must make sure that their writing is clear and easily understood by the reader. It is always advisable for a student to have a friend read your paper with the intent of ascertaining clarity. Often what seems clear to the writer will not be clear to another reader.

Cohesion

Cohesion refers to the way a paper flows from one idea to another. Another way of saying this is that cohesion has to do with the way the paper avoids skipping around from one idea to another unrelated idea. A writer who jumps from one idea to another without proper transition will end up with writing that confuses the reader.

The temptation exists, especially in published articles, for writers to attempt to make their writing seem to be at a higher academic level than is necessary. When the goal of writing is to impress rather than to inform or to communicate, there is a danger of ending up with a poor example of writing.

The student is cautioned to read carefully the rest of this book as a review of the essentials of the English language. There are times when the most experienced writer will need to refer to a style manual and to review a particular rule.

How to Construct a Paragraph

A paragraph is a group of sentences related together in some way. The parts of a paragraph are:
- The topic sentence (what the paragraph is about). Remember, a sentence is a group of words that express a complete thought. A sentence must have a subject (what the sentence is about) and a predicate (containing a verb).

When two or more sentences are run together without the proper punctuation the error is called a run-on sentence. Here is a sample run-on sentence: "The boys were chasing the giddy girls but they never caught them." This run-on sentence needs a comma after the word *girls*, because the sentence is made up of two independent clauses. An independent clause is a group of words that expresses a complete thought.
- Supporting sentences (These sentences build on the topic sentence).

• The transition sentence. At times the transition is obvious and doesn't need a contrived transition sentence. This is sometimes referred to as a summary sentence.

Sample Paragraphs

The following paragraphs were taken from the *Reader's Digest* and illustrate what might be considered a good paragraph. The reader can learn most about writing good paragraphs by reading the *Reader's Digest*, especially sections such as "Points to Ponder." Because *Reader's Digest* condenses articles, it is a very good example of brevity as a quality of good writing. Here are two sample paragraphs:

Ideas are the raw material of progress. Everything first takes shape in the form of an idea, but an idea by itself is worth nothing. An idea, like a machine, must have power applied to it before it can accomplish anything. The men who have won fame and fortune through having an idea are those who devoted every ounce of their strength and every dollar they could muster to putting it into operation. Ford had an idea, but he had to sweat and suffer and sacrifice in order to make it work. (Forbes)

A grammatical analysis of the above selection indicates:

Words per selection 92
Sentences 6
Words per sentence 15.3
Characters per word 4.2
Passive sentences 0
Reading level 8.7

"The road," wrote Cervantes, "is always better than the inn." Those who settle on fame or fortune as the inn, and having arrived, call it quits, miss the whole point of life. Realistically, there is no inn, no ultimate point of arrival. It is the road now and forever—finite man probing infinity, finding his way, endlessly. All that matters are the lessons learned along the way. (Leonard E. Read: *Meditations on Freedom;* Foundation for Economic Freedom.)

Words per selection 67
Sentences 5
Words per sentence 13.4
Characters per word 4.4
Passive sentences 0

Reading level 7.6

Conclusion

In each of the selections above it is obvious that the authors were not trying to impress people with their intellectual ability to write, but they were intent upon communicating ideas related to good writing. This should always be considered the main reason for writing—to communicate clearly.

Questions to Ask about a Paragraph and Headings

- Is each paragraph longer than a single sentence but not much longer than half a typed page?
- Do the levels of headings accurately reflect the organization of the paper?
- Are all the headings of the same level typed in the same format?
- Does the text under a particular heading reflect the topic only and accurately?

References in This Chapter

Aaron, J. E. (2002). *The Little, Brown Essential Handbook for Writers*. (4th ed.) New York: Longman.

Capitalization of Religious Terms

Abba
Advent, the
Advent season
age of grace
age to come, the
agnosticism
Almighty, the
almighty God
Alpha and Omega (Christ)
amillennial
ancient Near East
angel Gabriel, the
angel of the Lord, the
the Annunciation
Anointed One, the (Christ)
ante-Christian

antichrist (the spirit of the)
Antichrist (the person)
anti-Christian
anti-God
Apocalypse, the (Revelation of John)
apocalyptic
apostle Peter
apostles, the
Apostles' Creed
apostolic age
ark, the (Noah's)
ark of the covenant
Arminian(ism)
Ascension, the
atheism

baby Jesus, the
baptism
Battle of Armageddon
Beast, the (Antichrist)
Beatitudes, the
Betrayal, the
Bible school
blood of Christ
body of Christ (the church)
book of Genesis
Book of Life (book of judgment)
Bread of Life (Bible or Christ)
Calvary
Calvinist(ic), -ism
Canon, the (Scripture)
canon of Scripture, the
catholic (universal)
Catholic Church (Roman Catholic)
Catholicism
charismatic
charismatic movement
cherub(im)
chosen people (Jews)
Christ child
Christian era
church, the (body of Christ)
church (building)
church age
church fathers (the Fathers)
church triumphant
Comforter, the (Holy Spirit)
commandment (e.g., the first)
Commandments, the Ten
Communion (sacrament)
covenant, the
Creation, the (the act)
creation, the (the result)

Cross, the (the event)
cross, (the wooden object)
crown
Crucifixion, the
crucifixion of Christ
Day of Pentecost
deism, deist
Deity, the
deity of Christ
demon(ic)
devil, a
Devil, the (Satan)
disciples
dispensation(alism)(alist)
divine
Divine Father
early church
Eastern religions
ecumenism
end times, the
epistle to the Romans
Epistles, the
eschatology
eternal life
Eucharist
evangelical(s)
Exile, the
faith, the (Christianity)
Fall, the
fall of man
false christs
fatherhood of God
free will
fundamentalist(s), -ism
Garden of Eden
gehenna
General Epistles
Gentile, a
gentile laws

gnostic (generic)
Gnostic(ism) (specific sect)
God (Yahweh)
god (pagan)
godlike, godly
God's house
God's Word (the Bible)
God's word (his promise)
Golden Rule, the
Good News, the
good shepherd, the parable of the
gospel
gospel (e.g., John's gospel)
gospel of Mark
Gospels, the
gospel truth, the
grain offering
Great Commandment, the
hades
heaven (abode of the redeemed)
heavenly Father
hell
High Priest, the (Christ)
high priest, a
holiness
Holiness Movement, the
Holy Bible
Holy Book (Bible)
holy family
Holy Land (Palestine)
Holy of Holies
holy order(s)
Holy Roller
Holy Spirit
Holy Trinity
house of the Lord
Incarnation, the

incarnation of Christ
intertestamental
Jesus Prayer, the
John the Baptist
Judaic
Judeo-Christian
judges, the
Judgment Day
judgment seat of Christ
King James Version
kingdom, the
kingdom age
kingdom of God
kingdom of heaven
kingship of Christ
lake of fire
land of Canaan
Last Day, the
last days, the
law (as opposed to grace)
Law, the (Pentateuch)
liberal(ism)
living God
living Word, the (Bible)
Logos, the
Lord, the
lordship of Christ
Lord's Prayer, the
Lord's Supper, the
Magi
Major Prophets, the (OT books)
major prophets (people)
mammon
Man, the (Jesus)
Messiah, the (Christ)
messiahship
messianic
millennial kingdom

Millennium, the
Mosaic
Mosaic Law
name of Christ, the
Nativity, the
nativity of Christ, the
Near East
neo-pentecostalism
new heaven and new earth
Nicene Creed
Nicene fathers
Ninety-five Theses
non-Christian
only begotten Son of God
orthodox(y)
parable of the prodigal son
paradise (heaven)
Paradise (Garden of Eden)
partial Rapture
Pastoral Epistles
Paul the apostle
Pauline Epistles
Paul's epistles
Pentecost
Pentecostal(ism)
person of Christ
(the three) persons of the
    Trinity
Pharaoh (when used as name
without article)
pharaoh, the (general)
pharisaic (attitude)
Pharisaic (if in reference to
  Pharisees)
Pharisee
pillar of clouds
pope, the
Pope John Paul II
postbiblical

post-Christian
predestination
premillennial
Prodigal Son, the
prophet Isaiah, the
prophets, the (people)
Prophets, the (OT books)
Protestant(ism)
Providence (God)
providence of God
providential
Psalm 119
Psalms, the (the OT book)
psalm, a
psalmist, the
rabbi
Rapture, the
Redeemer, the
Reformation, the
Reformed theology
Resurrection, the
resurrection of Christ
sacrament(s)
Satan
satanic
satanism
Savior
scriptural
Scripture(s) (Bible; n. and
    adj.)
scripture(s) (other religions)
Second Adam (Christ)
Second Coming, the
second coming of Christ
Septuagint
Sermon on the Mount
Serpent, the (Satan)
Seventh-day Adventist
shalom

Solomon's temple
Son of God
Son of Man
Sovereign Lord
Sunday school
synagogue
tabernacle, the (OT building)
temple, the (at Jerusalem)
temptation of Christ, the
ten tribes of Israel, the
Testaments, the
tomb, the
Transfiguration, the
tribe of Judah
Tribulation, the (historical event)

Trinitarian
Trinity, the
Triumphal Entry
triune God
Twelve, the
twelve apostles, the
Twenty-third Psalm
unchristian
ungodly
unscriptural
vacation Bible school
Way, the Truth, and the Life
wise men, the
Word made flesh (Christ)
Yahweh
Yuletide

CHAPTER SIX
Formatting: Margins, Spacing, and Such

Formal research reports follow prescribed rules for format and style that set them apart from other types of presentation. This text shows examples of those rules, but is itself designed with much more variety in many matters—layout and typefaces, for example—so that it is not a pattern of the formal requirements. It will save you a great amount of time later if you follow the format and style requirements from the beginning.

Margins

Set margins for one inch top, bottom, left, and right.

Justification

In page layout, "justification" refers to the alignment of the words at the margin. The custom for academic papers and formal business reports is left justification only.

Font

Use either Times New Roman or Arial, or a precise equivalent, in 12 point. Use the same typeface and size throughout the paper with the exception of superscripts or subscripts, if needed.

Vertical Spacing

Double space throughout, including References, except for multi-line titles or headings. Every page begins one inch from the top of the paper.

Indentation

Indent new paragraphs half an inch. The operational definitions and references have a half-inch hanging indent because they are alphabetized.

Italics and Underlines

Forget about these features. Never use either to add emphasis; strengthen your writing by your choice of words, not by typography. Italics are used to denote titles of creative works (especially in References) and to denote a foreign word. Underlining is not used.

Page Numbers

Arabic numerals are used throughout, starting with 2 on the second sheet. Place at the top right margin, .5 inch below the edge of the paper.

The Use of Abbreviations

Spell out names and terms the first time used in each chapter, followed by the abbreviation (abbr.) in parentheses. Thereafter you may use just the abbr. Abbreviations do not require apostrophes unless in the possessive form. For example: The two RNs discussed the 1960's. The landing on the moon may have been the 1960's most triumphant moment. The administrator docked the RNs' pay because of their loafing. (Possessive form: RNs' plural; RN's singular.)

Type of Paper

Regular 20# white stock is suitable. You may use a premium, rag content stock if you prefer, but it is not required. Print on one side only.

When to Start a New Page

Begin at the top of a new page for each section, such as Table of Contents, chapters, References, and appendixes. Each section such as these will have a level 1 heading, 1 inch below the top of the paper.

Headings

Headings will follow the format shown here and used in the examples. You probably will use only the chapter head and levels two and three. It is a very simple system:

CHAPTER HEADINGS (LEVEL 1) ALL CAPS, BOLD, CENTERED

Level Two: Caps and Lower Case, Bold, Centered

Level Three: Caps and Lower Case, Centered

Level Four: Caps and Lower Case, Bold, Left Justified

Long Headings or Titles

Headings can usually be kept to one line. If necessary, break at a logical place so the second line is shorter than the first line, and single space, as done in the chapter example just above. Multi-line titles and headings are single spaced.

Format of Back Matter Headings

Headings for front-matter and back matter are all caps, bold, centered, as:

APPENDIX A: RAW DATA

This style applies to References, all Appendixes (identified by letter and title as shown above), Bibliography, and Index (the latter two being optional and rarely needed).

Title Page

If the title requires more than one line, subsequent lines are single spaced, and each line is shorter than the line above it. The title page does not have a page number.

Certification Page

Follow the sample in the appendix. Sign it before submission.

Abstract

The abstract is presented in conventional text format (justified left only, double spaced, paragraphs indented one-half inch. The heading is centered, bold, all caps.

Table of Contents

Follow the format used in the sample in the appendix. To justify the right hand margin and insert leaders, click **Format**, click **Tabs.** Set **Tab Stop Position** at 6.5 inches, choose **Alignment Right** and **Leader 2.** Click **Set**. Click **Okay**. You're all set!

List of Figures or List of Tables

Each will go on a new page. Use the same format as used for the Table of Contents. Provide only if there are more than five entries.

Placement of Tables and Figures

In the report, tables should be placed as close to the narrative as possible. Figures are not to be more than 3 inches high.

References

Double-space throughout. Provide a half inch hanging indent. See Chapter 7 for more details. (*Many* more details!)

CHAPTER SEVEN

Documentation: References, Footnotes, and Such

When you assert statements of fact you need to document the source. This occurs most frequently in Chapter 2, but the requirements and procedures apply throughout the proposal and report. The method of documentation in the text (the chapters) is the parenthetical citation. This is backed up by the detailed list, References, which appears just after Chapter 5.

All information gathered from books, periodicals, websites, interviews, or by any other means must be identified in the text of the report and in References in the back matter. Note two small words in that sentence: *all* and *must*. It is not difficult—if you keep track as you go. (More small words of great importance: *if you keep track as you go.*)

Documentation establishes your credibility by gathering agreement from individuals or organizations readers have reason to believe are authoritative, which is why the bulk of your documentation should come from scholarly, peer-reviewed journals.

Definitions

Define major variables, concepts, or terms that are specific to this study or are new or novel to the reader. Define important terms that may have multiple definitions and need to be clarified. Document as needed. Write the definition in complete sentences.

Introduce the words that will be defined, i.e.. Grant (2002), in his thesis under the heading definitions stated the following:

• *Kansas high school science teachers* are defined as those who teach one or more of their courses in science for grades 9-12 within the state of Kansas.

• A *worldview* is "an ideology, philosophy, theology, movement, or religion that provides an overarching approach to understanding God and His world, or a set of presuppositions (assumptions which may be true, partially true, or entirely false) which we hold (consciously or subconsciously, consistently or inconsistently) about the makeup of our world" (Smithwick & Woods, 1996. p. 14). A worldview acts as a filter of incoming ideas, facts, information, arguments, and other evidences. This worldview filter allows a person to determine what may be accepted as reality, and what should be dismissed as foolishness.

• A *belief* is a state of mind in which trust or confidence is placed in something, or the conviction of the truth of some statement, especially when based on examination of evidence. (Mish, et al., 1985)

• *Teaching practices* are classroom instruction methods initiated and facilitated by the teacher with the purpose of assisting the students in gaining understanding of the items surveyed.

Documentation Within the Text

Short Direct Quotations

A quotation consisting of fewer than forty words should be incorporated into the text (APA, 2001, p. 292). It should be enclosed in quotation marks and combined smoothly as part of your own sentence. The source of the quotation is identified by a parenthetical citation.

Example, One Author: No one really believes that a pastor's job is easy, but it surprises some people that "dealing with volunteer leaders may be the hardest part of ministering to a congregation" (Anthony, 1993, p. 44).
   Note the format of the citation: author, year, and page number.

If Two Authors: Use both names every time, joined by an ampersand.
   (Walters & DeKoven, 2007, p. 58)

If Three, Four, or Five Authors: Use all authors' names the first time; only the first author after that.
   First time: (Hoople, Smith, Begley, & Wamser, 2006, p. 92)
   Subsequently it is just: (Hoople, et al., 2006, p. 94)

If Six or More Authors: Always just the last name of the first author. If a work was written by Anchor, Brown, Cosky, Drebben, Elias, & Fenwick, the citation is always just: (Anchor, et al., 2007, p. 15).

Long Direct Quotations

A quotation consisting of more than forty words should be set off from the rest of the paper by the following procedure:
   • double space above and below the quotation

- the quotation itself is double spaced
- indent the quoted material ½ inch from the left (as in the example below)
- do not use quotation marks; the extra indentation is sufficient to indicate that the passage is quoted.
- keep long quotations to a minimum

Example of a Long Quotation

> Whether we label the relating of the Bible and psychology as "integration" or as "interface" of psychology and theology or the "relationship" of faith and learning is not our main concern. What is important is the concept of wrestling with the relationship between the findings of psychology and the revelation of the Bible. ... We believe there is a biblical imperative for every Christian who works with people—be it from the pulpit or in the classroom, laboratory, or counseling office—to come to grips with an understanding of the human being that is as comprehensive as possible (Carter & Narramore, 1979, p. 16).

In a manuscript, the quote is indented one-half inch from the left and is double-spaced. All quotations, long or short, must be referenced by a parenthetical citation to identify the source.

Documentation of Paraphrased Material

It is often a better use of space and of a reader's time to paraphrase rather than quote directly. This is fully acceptable when done accurately, and can allow your writing to flow more smoothly. Page numbers are not required for paraphrased material, but name and date should appear where credit is due.

Reference Citations in Text

To refer to an item in the list of references from the text, an author-date method should be used. That is, use the surname of the author (without suffixes) and the year of the publication in the text at appropriate points.

One author

Isaac (2001) indicated in his research ...

Findings in a recent study (Isaac, 2001), indicate that ...

Two or more authors

When a work has two authors, always cite both names every time the reference occurs. For works with three, four, or five authors, cite all authors the first time the reference occurs. In subsequent citations, include only the last name of the first author followed by *et al.*

When a Work Has No Authors

Cite in text the first few words of what appears first for the entry on the list (usually the title) and the year.

How to Include an Internet Address In The Text

It is generally better to avoid including an Internet address (a URL) in the body of a work because they are often cumbersome and slow down the flow of the reader's comprehension. Include them if you think it better, following these rules:

- Do not underline it.
- Have it print in black.
- Avoiding breaking it into two lines. If it is so long that it will not fit on one line, break it just after a slash (/) but do not add a hyphen.
- If the URL ends the sentence, do not add a period.

Where To Put The Parenthetical Citation

If the author of the original material is mentioned in the paragraph using the quoted material, it may be done as: DeKoven (1988) suggested that "all marriages can be somewhat dysfunctional from time to time."

If the author's name is not used in the sentence it must be in the citation, as: "The literature as a whole seems to agree with the basic concept of the widespread occasion of dysfunction in American families since the end of the Vietnam war" (DeKoven, 1988).

If the parenthetical citation is at the end of the quote, the citation follows the closing quotation mark and the period is at the end of the sentence.

Footnotes

The current APA style and practice (2001, p. 202) is to use footnotes for content and copyright permission. They can be a distraction to readers, and they can complicate the task of word processing. Use them sparingly.

When to Use a Footnote

• Only when it is important to supplement or amplify textual information. A footnote should address only one topic. They should not contain material such as graphs, charts, or extensive formulas.
• When the author needs to acknowledge the source of copyrighted material a footnote is appropriate (APA, 2001, p. 202).

How to Set up Footnotes

• Number footnotes consecutively throughout the paper.
• In the text, place the number slightly above the line at the end of the of the material to be acknowledged. No period follows the number.
• Unless the writer is using a computer program that automatically inserts footnotes, the following method should be used:
   1. Place the number (again, above the line and without a period) along with its footnote at the bottom of the page. Indent the first line of each footnote and start the second line even with the left margin.
   2. Draw a line from margin to margin to separate the footnotes from the body of the paper.
   3. Use single-spacing for footnotes that require more than one line.

The Reference List

Academic research at all levels requires identification of all books, journal articles, and information from any source that is quoted or paraphrased in the project. It must supply an "address" that will enable another person to locate the source of your information. This list, bearing the caption, References, will appear following the text and before any appendices.

Double space throughout. Degrees and first names are not indicated either in References or in parenthetical citations. In the examples below, notice that in book and journal titles only the first word, the first word after a colon, and proper names are capitalized. Also, notice what may seem like unnecessary periods after parentheses. Include them! This will guide you through most situations, but consult the *Publication Manual of the APA* (2001) for other circumstances.

Everything listed in References must be used somewhere in the body of the paper and every parenthetical citation in the paper must be given in References. Before you submit a paper or report, go through it from start to finish to look at each parenthetical citation, and to then check References to see if it is there. If it is, put either a check mark beside the listing in References or make a note at the proper spot to add it. When you have gone all through the report, see if you have any entries in References that do not have a check mark. If you do, either delete it (it doesn't belong because you didn't use it) or see if you may have missed it when you went through the first time.

An example set of references with the type identified is shown below. Page and item numbers from the APA manual are in parentheses. Use this only as a reference and general guide to the simplest types of entries.

Book with one author (248, B)

Eickson, M. J. (2001). *Truth or consequences: The promise and perils of postmodernism.* Downers Grove, IL: InterVarsity Press.

Book with multiple authors (248, 23)

Vickers, R. J. & Porter, P. H. (2007). *Men start here: 199 ideas and suggestions to honor and love your wife.* Warrensburg, MO: Artful Askers.

Edited book (249, 26)

Wainwright, G. & Tucker, K. B. W. (Eds.). (2006). *The Oxford history of Christian worship.* New York: Oxford University Press.

Article or chapter in an edited book (252, 34)

Egbulem, N. C. (2006). Mission and Inculturation: Africa. In G. Wainwright & K. B. W. Tucker (Eds.), *The Oxford history of Christian worship* (pp. 678-695). New York: Oxford University Press.

Article or book produced by an organization, without an author's name (249, 6)

Department of Consumer Safety. (2005). *How to choose non-hazardous toys for infants.* Washington, DC: U. S. Government Printing Office.

Journal article, one author (240, 1)

Emerson, M. (1996). Through tinted glasses: Religion, worldviews, and abortion attitudes. *Journal for the Scientific Study of Religion, 35* (1), 41-45.

Journal article, two authors (240, 2)

Allen, N. & Crawley, F. (1998). Voices form the bridge: Worldview conflicts of Kickapoo students of science. *Journal of Research in Science Teaching, 35,* 111-132.

Journal article three to six authors (240, 3)

Rogers, J. R., Bromley, J. L., McNally, C. J., & Lester, D. (2007). Content analysis of suicide notes as a test of the motivational component of the existential-constructivist model of suicide. *Journal of Counseling & Development, 85,* 182-188.

Monthly publication no author (not shown in APA)

Gallup Poll Monthly, (2007, September). 28.

Encyclopedia or Dictionary (250, 30)

Giesler, N. (Ed.). (1999). *Baker encyclopedia of Christian apologetics.* Grand Rapids: Baker.

Magazine article, one author (241, 6)

Kantrowitz, B. (2007, Oct. 15). In all their glory: Women and power. *Newsweek, 150,* 47.

Newsletter article (242, 7)

Westing, E. Z. (2007, Spring) REM sleep improves when conscience is relieved of neurotic conflicts. *Wellness 4U Today, 15,* 20.

Newspaper article, no author (242, 9)

Prayer: The history of one of mankind's oldest practices. (2005, Dec 25). *The Washington Times.* p. B8.

Unpublished thesis (262, 57)

Bierma, T. W. (2007). *Cultural exegesis for transformational preaching.* Unpublished master's thesis, Calvin Theological Seminary, Grand Rapids, MI.

Unpublished doctoral dissertation (262, 56)

Rees, S. (2007). *Discovering the equippers among us: Using behavior-based interviews for identifying, drawing out, and nurturing the equipping leaders of Ephesians 4:11.* Unpublished doctoral dissertation, Western Theological Seminary, Holland, MI.

Entry in an Encyclopedia (254, 38)

Imago. (2000). In *World Book Encyclopedia* (Vol. 10, p. 79). Chicago: World Book Encyclopedia.

Video or motion picture (266, 65)

Allen, L. (Director), & Strobel, L. (Writer). 2006. *The Case for a creator.* (DVD). LaHabra, CA: Illustra Media. (Available from Amazon.com).

Unpublished paper presented at a meeting (260, 529)

Svigel, M. J. (2002, March) *P46 as the earliest witness of 1 Thessalonians 2:13-16.* Paper presented at the Southwestern Regional meeting of the Evangelical Theological Society, Dallas, TX.

Electronic Formats

Internet article based on print source

A citation is done as if it were a paper article, followed by a retrieval statement that identifies the date retrieved and source.

Cha, P. T. (2006). Faithful generations: Race and new Asian American churches. *Journal for the Scientific Study of Religion, 45,* 628-629. Retrieved October 12, 2007, from Proquest.

Web page, no date

Thompson, G. (n.d.). Youth coach handbook. In *Joe soccer*.
Retrieved September 17, 2001 from
http://www.joesoccer.com/menu.html

Web page, government author

Wisconsin Department of Natural Resources. (2001, March 14).
Glacial habitat restoration areas. Retrieved September 18, 2001
from http://www.dnr.state.wi.us/org/land/wildlife/hunVhra.htm

Web page, no author, no date

Eldorado, (n.d.). In PlacesNamed.com. Retrieved September 18,
2001 from http://www.placesnamed.com/e/l/eldorado.asp

Personal communications (214, 3.102)

Personal communications may be things such as email messages,
speeches, interviews, and telephone conversations. Because the
information is not retrievable by others they do not appear in the
reference list but are cited within the text, as follows:

J. Burnitz (personal communications, September 20, 2007).

The Annotated Reference List

At times a student will be asked to include an annotated set of
references in an assignment. The annotated reference list is labeled as
such and is no less than a reference, as in the example above, but with
a short annotation or summary of the source.

Example of an Entry in an Annotated Reference

Moberg, D. O. (Ed.). (2001). *Aging and spirituality: Spiritual
dimensions of aging theory, research, practice, and policy.* New
York: Haworth Pastoral Press.
Broad exploration of such questions as: Are spirituality and religion
the same? Is spirituality outside the domain of scientific research?
How is spiritual care relevant to the helping professions? How can we
evaluate or measure spiritual wellness? Essays are grouped into four
sections: Conceptual and Theoretical Foundations; Research and
Spirituality; Professional and Practical Applications; Policy Implications and Priorities for the Future.

Some General Rules for APA Reference Pages

• Begin the reference list on a new page. The page begins with the word "References" ("Reference" if there is only one), centered in the top, middle of the page, using upper case. If the references take up more than one page, do not re-type the word "References" on sequential pages, simply continue your list.

• Use one space after all punctuation.

• The first line of the reference is flush left. Lines thereafter are indented as a group, ½ inch, to create a hanging indention.

• Double space throughout.

• Use italics for titles of books, newspapers, magazines, and journals.

• References cited in text must appear in the reference list; conversely, each entry in the reference list must be cited in text.

• Arrange entries in alphabetical order.

• Give in parentheses the year the work was published. For magazines and newspapers, give the year followed by the month and date, if any. If no date is available, write n.d.

• Give volume numbers for magazines, journals, and newsletters. Include the issue number for journals only if each issue begins on a page 1.

Examples

The examples in this section will be instructive to you but they should not substitute for your consultation with requirements stated in written form. Also, since projects vary widely, the examples illustrate only the most important rules of form and style. The examples are from several projects; they do not relate to one another.

> **Title Page:** The elements to be included are as shown, centered. Only the title is in bold. Begin the title 2" below the top of the page, the next blocks 5" and 8" below the top of the page.

**THE TITLE IS IN ALL CAPS, SINGLE SPACED,
CENTERED HORIZONTALLY, AND
TWO INCHES BELOW THE
TOP OF THE PAGE**

Submitted for Course
OT505
The Book of Psalms

by
Dana J. Student
0000 Address Street
Hometown, State 00000
January 00, 0000

Certification Page (For thesis or dissertation only.) Start at top margin and use vertical spacing approximately as shown here.

CERTIFICATION PAGE

This is to certify that the project prepared

By Dana J. Student

Entitled: *Name Of The Project In Title Capitalization Form*

Has been accepted by the faculty of Vision International University.

Signed:

Project Advisor_____

Date _____ Final Grade _____

Abstract: An abstract is an unbiased summary—250 words maximum—of the project's purpose, methods of investigation, and findings. Use same format for **Preface** or **Acknowledgements.**

ABSTRACT

Evaluations of change and satisfaction six months after counseling in a church-based lay counseling program were obtained for two groups of clients (N = 55, 43). The lay counselors compared favorably with Family Service Association professionals on measures of client change and satisfaction. Statistical analysis yielded information useful in management of the program and supervision of lay counselors. This article provides a model for follow-up process that can be used by other lay counseling programs.

Dedication: This is not common but may be included in a thesis or dissertation. A more conventional method is to include personal remarks in a Preface or Acknowledgement.

DEDICATION

To my parents, who modeled

compassion in parenting,

excellence in vocation,

and joyful obedience in Christian living.

90

> **Table of Contents:** Start at top margin; use vertical spacing, capitalization, and bold as shown. The example is from a project of empirical research. Within chapters, use headings to fit your topic.

TABLE OF CONTENTS

List of Tables or List of Figures: Use only if the report contains more than five tables or figures

LIST OF TABLES

The first page of any chapter: Do not include any extra vertical spacing. (Single space only in multiple-line titles or headings.) The first paragraph of every chapter introduces the chapter by concisely summarizing (previewing) its content.

CHAPTER 2: LITERATURE REVIEW

This chapter will reveal different methods in which patient satisfaction has been reviewed and improved. Various medical facilities have been analyzed for their innovative attempts to improve their customer satisfaction and gain insight into the customer's expectation level.

Sources Consulted

Websites such as Aunt Minnie.com, Nurseweek.com, WebMD, and Google searches for customer satisfaction were explored. The Bryan College Library provided many periodicals through ProQuest and JStor.

Film Star Treatment

Hoosier Radiology in Fort Wayne, Indiana treats its customers like humans, not numbers, according to Dr. Raymond Gize, founder (Diaz, 1992). The waiting room boasts of personal items from staff members and physicians, such as a circa 1930 Mediterranean-style hutch. The personal touches of artwork and the ancestral home-like atmosphere lend a comforting air to an otherwise anxiety-ridden waiting room. The founder of the facility, Dr. Raymond Gize, focuses on every staff member being patient oriented. Little things can make a difference in patient satisfaction, such as stopping to talk to a patient. While equipment is important to Dr. Gize, one of the things he values most is a letter of gratitude from a young patient's mother, who thanked him for going out of his way to care for her child.

Soothing Pediatric Waiting Room

A mix of cartoon spaceships, animated floral scenes, and geometric patterns has a calming effect on the young patients at Advocate Lutheran General Children's Hospital in Park Ridge, Illinois (Anastos & Campbell, 2006). The children arriving in the waiting area are given a tablet PC and a radiofrequency identification (RFID) card. The child chooses a theme from a

12

Figure within the text: A bar graph, placed immediately after the hypothesis to which it relates. There was not enough room on the page for Figure 2, so it is placed as near as it could be, which is at the top of the next page (not shown).

Date Relating to the Hypotheses

Hypothesis 1

Adult female members of First Church will indicate a more positive attitude toward worship services than will adult male members, as measured by responses to items 5-10 of the Melton Religious Attitudes Survey (MRAS).

Figure 1: Mean Scores, Attitude Toward Worship

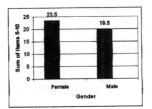

Items 5-10 of the MRAS queried about attitudes toward the worship experience at First Church. Hypothesis 1 was tested by comparing the mean of the sums of scores for the 6 items (5-10). Males reported a mean of 21.0 and females a mean level of 24.5, as shown in Figure 1. Hypothesis 1 was supported by the data.

Hypothesis 2

Adult female members of First Church will indicate a more positive attitude toward Sunday adult education than will adult male members, as measured by responses to items 11-16 of the MRAS.

Items 11-16 of the MRAS queried about attitudes toward Sunday adult education at First Church. Hypothesis 2 was tested by comparing the mean of the sums of scores for the 6 items (11-16). Males reported a mean of 23.7 and females a mean level of 19.9, as shown in Figure 2. Hypothesis 2 was not supported by the data.

94

Analysis of Data

Hypothesis 1

Hypothesis 1 stated: "Students taught by a specialized phonics program will produce greater academic reading achievement than classroom students taught by traditional classroom reading techniques."

There were 20 students in both the control group that utilized only the county adopted literacy program and the experimental groups. Throughout the school year all the children in each classroom were given standardized testing to monitor their improvement in the areas of Nonsense Word Fluency, Phoneme Segmentation and Oral Reading Fluency (definitions of these are given in the glossary). Although all three were monitored, only Oral Reading Fluency was used to test Hypothesis 1.

The treatment group had a mean Oral Reading Fluency score of 59.7 in September, of 92.5 in May, a net increase of 32.8, or 55 percent. The control group had a mean Oral Reading Fluency score of 60.3 in September, of 85.6 in May, a net increase of 25.3, or 42 percent. These data are shown in Table 4. Hypothesis 1 was supported.

Table 4: Mean Oral Reading Fluency Scores in September and May

Group	Sept.	May	Score Change	% Change
Treatment Group	59.7	92.5	32.8	55.
Control Group	60.3	85.6	25.3	42

Hypothesis 2

Hypothesis 2 stated: Girls in both classrooms will produce greater academic reading achievement than boys in those classrooms.

Again, Oral Reading Fluency was used as the evaluative measure. The girls in the

References: Do not rely on this example alone, but get more complete guidance from within this text or from the APA Publications Manual. Only the first page has a heading.

REFERENCES

Califf, R.M., Morse, M., Wittes, J., Goodman, S.N., Nelson, D.K., & DeMets, D.L.
(2003). Toward protecting the safety of participants in clinical trials.
Controlled Clinical Trials, 24, 256-271.

DeMarinis, A. (2004, January-February). Sponsor inspections: What, why, and
how. *Research Practitioner, 5*(1), 12-21.

Emannel, E. (2004). Oversight of human participant research: Identifying
problems to evaluate reform proposals. *Annals of Internal Medicine, 141,*
282-291.

Emard, E. (2004, September-October). The partnership for human research
protection: Setting the standard for safety. *Research Practitioner, 5*(5), 157-
160.

Federman, D. D., Hanna, K. E., & Rodriguez, L. L. (Eds.). (2002). *Responsible
research: A systems approach to protecting research participants.*
Washington, DC: National Academies Press.

Jamrozik, K. (2000). The case for a new system for oversight of research on
human subjects. *Journal of Medical Ethics, 26,* 334-339.

Koph, J., Murtha, L., & Jaffe, R. (2004, December). IRBs prove to be a vital cog
in human research compliance. *Clinical Trials Compliance, 3*(12), 1.

Lillypad, M. O., & Frogge, W. W. (2001). *Monitoring ethical behavior in medial
research.* Chicago: Buckram and Bristol Press.

Mandelbaum, J. J. & Grimes, R. F. (2007). The lability of reciprocal decay in
viscous transfer anodes. *Journal of Entoprenal Physics, 7,* 7-28.

Raw Data: Because empirical studies vary greatly, you may decide how data are presented. Here the data have been put into a new table. Raw data may be shown as they appeared in a database.

APPENDIX A: RAW DATA

Phoneme Segmentation Fluency

First Grade Classroom A: Traditional Instruction

Student ID #, Gender	Score, Sept 2004	Score, Jan 2005	Interval Change	Score, May 2005	Interval Change	Total Change
01 – B	50	50	0	46	-4	-4
02 – G	49	61	12	63	2	14
03 – G	45	54	9	67	13	22
04 – G	34	51	17	61	10	27
05 – B	53	54	1	74	20	21
06 – B	61	54	-7	55	1	-6
07 – B	48	73	25	70	-3	22
08 – G	46	53	7	61	8	15
09 – B	42	56	14	65	9	23
10 – B	29	44	15	50	6	21
11 – G	48	64	16	70	6	22
12 – B	55	62	7	64	2	9
13 – G	46	58	12	69	11	23
14 – B	48	57	9	61	4	13
15 – B	74	57	-17	70	13	-4
16 – B	17	39	22	33	-6	16
17 – G	43	48	5	60	12	17
18 – G	57	na	na	52	-5	-5

Shaded row = Exceptional Education student

Instrument: Show materials used in the project. It is better to scan for inclusion, as was done here; attach actual materials or photos only if there is no other way.

APPENDIX B: INSTRUMENT

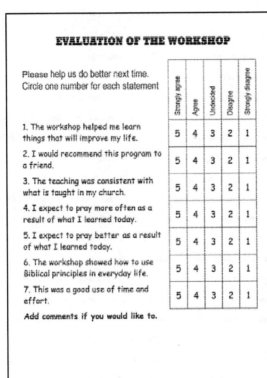

EVALUATION OF THE WORKSHOP

Please help us do better next time.
Circle one number for each statement

	Strongly agree	Agree	Undecided	Disagree	Strongly disagree
1. The workshop helped me learn things that will improve my life.	5	4	3	2	1
2. I would recommend this program to a friend.	5	4	3	2	1
3. The teaching was consistent with what is taught in my church.	5	4	3	2	1
4. I expect to pray more often as a result of what I learned today.	5	4	3	2	1
5. I expect to pray better as a result of what I learned today.	5	4	3	2	1
6. The workshop showed how to use Biblical principles in everyday life.	5	4	3	2	1
7. This was a good use of time and effort.	5	4	3	2	1

Add comments if you would like to.

Sample paper: Margins are 1 inch all around. Two-line titles and headings are single-spaced.

THE PREVALENCE OF MALE HOMOSEXUALITY
IN THE AMERICAN COLLEGE STUDENT

Introduction

A recent *Union-Tribune* article reported that only 2% of American males admitted to being homosexual (Monday, April 22, 1993). These data differ from the findings of the Masters and Johnson study of a few years ago where the percentage was claimed to be much higher. From all of the attention on homosexuality being focused upon in the media, it would seem that the percentage of men involved in a homosexual lifestyle is not diminishing, but increasing.

Studies by Hoffman (1968), Kinsey, Pomeroy, Martin and Gebbert (1948), Teal (1971), and others, offer conflicting statistics. This suggests that there may be a problem in the methodology used in the research by some of the authors in this field of study.

Indeed, it was revealed (Maslow, 1952) that Kinsey's methods had been criticized by the noted psychologist, Maslow, before they were published. Subsequent disclosures in 1982 by Kinsey's co-author, Pomeroy, indicated that Kinsey's data were seriously skewed as a result of faulty, if not deliberately biased, methods (Leavitt, 1991).

A study that would be conducted in a scientifically designed research format, rather than a simple one-on-one interview or by questionnaire, seems to be indicated in order to arrive at a more accurate study of this issue. A design for such a study is described in this paper.

The Problem

The personal interview and/or the questionnaire method of research has been the most common method of arriving at statistics in the area of human sexuality but these methods seem to produce conflicting results. It is reasonable to assume that the subject in personal interviews may hesitate to be completely honest when discussing his sexual life style. When the interview or questionnaire methods are used, some subjects may be tempted to exaggerate or be less than

99

2

completely truthful, for whatever reason. This indicates a need for a more reliable and valid

research design in order to ensure an accurate picture of the prevalence of homosexuality.

Background

Many people are hesitant to fully discuss their sexual preferences, especially with a

professional researcher who may be viewed as a psychologist. The studies keep appearing in the

literature from time to time with differing results. Some of the earliest studies concentrated on

the concept of latent homosexuality.

There seems to be an increase in the occurrence of homosexuality among members of the

clergy and among other Christian church members. Most Christian counselors are ill-equipped

to deal with problems in this area, in part because they have not been able to study the problem

from reliable, valid research.

The Purpose

The purpose of this study will be to determine a more reliable and valid statistic

regarding the prevalence of homosexuality among American college males.

Significance

Significant research into the possible treatment modalities for the problem of

homosexuality (and other sexual dysfunctions) cannot be achieved until reliable and valid

research findings are available. Any social problem can only be studied for possible resolution if

the statistics regarding the problem are accurate and there are research methods available to

arrive at statistically valid results.

The Nature of the Study

The study will use the methodology of correlation research. Previous studies that have

been completed will be analyzed statistically to determine the validity and reliability of the

References to Works Cited in This Book

American Psychological Association. (2001). *Publication manual of the American Psychological Association* (5th ed.). Washington, DC: American Psychological Association.

Ary, D., Jacobs, L. G., Razavieh, A., & Sorenson, C. K. (2007). *Introduction to research in education* (7th ed.). Belmont, CA: Wadsworth.

Charles, C. (1998). *Introduction to educational research.* NY: Longman.

Grant, D. (2002). *Beliefs and teaching practices of Kansas high school science teachers in relation to creation and evolution worldviews.* Unpublished thesis, Institute for Creation Research, Santee, CA.

How to Succeed in Independent Study

The emphasis at Vision International University is on the individual within a community. The heart of such an approach to education is the personal relationship between a student and the adviser/coordinator and mentor assigned to him or her. The mentor helps the student plan and coordinate a course of study. Besides providing instruction in their own fields of specialization, mentors advise students about the academic alternatives open to them, assist students in designing their academic programs, identify instructional resources, and evaluate the overall quality of each student's work. As you progress in your program at VIU, keep in contact with your mentor and work closely with them on your writing projects.

Independent Study Is Unique

Independent study is planned and organized by the University. The learning system allows students to study at convenient times, places, and at a pace suited to student needs. While independent study offers great flexibility and freedom from fixed schedules, it also requires *commitment, maturity,* and *motivation* on the part of the student. The student should ask for an honest evaluation of something written early in their program. If weak areas are identified, the necessary steps to correct them can be implemented.

Individual Study Plans

Vision International University is committed to the idea that effective learning is based on purposes and needs that are important to the individual, that learning occurs in varied places, and that different people learn in different ways. Students are encouraged and expected to plan and design studies that help them clarify their purposes and acquire the competence, knowledge, and awareness necessary to pursue those purposes actively and independently. Students choose their courses according to their interests and in the context of general University expectations for academic study. Students may study traditional subjects in a traditional manner, or they may choose an innovative degree program and incorporate various non-traditional modes of study.

Issues Specific to Graduate Students

For those students enrolled in a graduate program it is wise to have a plan and to know your purpose for seeking the graduate degree of your choice. You should choose the program that is right for your needs. If you plan to do doctoral work, you should choose a Masters program which requires the writing of a thesis. If you are only interested in the Masters and not a doctorate, a thesis is not as important. Currently the Masters programs at *VIU* do not require a thesis, however a student may opt to write one. For more information about this important decision, contact *VIU*.

Some Problems of Independent Learning

Not all adult students will have the same kinds of problems. Some of the most common ones are listed here:

• Adult students may lack confidence in their ability to learn, especially if they have little contact with other students working on the same program.

• As a result they may be fearful of not doing well and feel they will lose face if their work is not perfect. This may cause delay in submitting work for comments and guidance.

• They are anxious about how to combine their studies with the demands of family, friends, neighbors, employers, and working colleagues. They may feel guilty about spending time shut up alone with books.

• They may, quite simply, feel too tired after a hard day's work to make the transition to mental effort.

• They may not possess adequate writing or study skills.

The Adult Student Has Several Advantages

Adult students have more experience, more knowledge and, above all, more motivation than most non-adult students. While adult students may find that their memory is not as good as that of younger people, they are likely to be better at grasping and analyzing the underlying principles and relationships among the principles. This kind of understanding is far more valuable in higher education than mere knowledge of facts. Research on distance education is abundant now, and it clearly shows that adult students learning at a distance can do just as well as younger students who are working in a classroom.

Vision International University students enjoy advantages that are denied to other students who are doing undergraduate or graduate work by correspondence, as Vision International University is breaking new ground in program planning, in presentation, and in follow-up, with the needs of specific students in mind. Vision offers the following types of courses: traditional correspondence, video and audio based, on-line, and teacher-taught and led seminars.

Vision International University students will seldom get a chance to feel forgotten or isolated. With the help of our student services, we provide encouragement, guidance about how to learn, and feedback about student progress.

Working Effectively

There are really no secrets to success for an adult student learning at a distance. Study is hard and demanding work. There are no tricks or short cuts that can make it easy. But what we must aim to do is ensure that your hard work does produce results—that is, *effective* and *rewarding* work. To be an effective student you will need the following:

1. Clear and realistic goals. Whether you are studying for career advancement, to broaden and illuminate your everyday life, or to equip yourself to cooperate more with others, you must identify both short-term goals and long-term goals that can give urgency to all your work (e.g., completing an assignment, attaining skills, starting on a new career).

2. Support from those close to you. You no doubt have many roles besides that of student—spouse, parent, friend, employee. When an adult first returns to study, it can be a difficult time for husband or wife and for the children. This needs to be faced beforehand, with a necessary re-allocation of duties and responsibilities being openly discussed and decided. If the others share your goals and progress, the going will be so much easier.

3. A business-like approach. Many successful students would argue that good organization rather than academic brilliance is the key to

good progress in their studies. You will be less anxious about your work if you try to:

- Plan what you want to achieve in the next day, week, month.

- Stick to your plans, or modify them only for good reasons.

- Make the best possible use of available spare time.

- Realize that you must sacrifice something in order to find time for the course.

- Pray about your plans. "The plans of the diligent lead surely to advantage" (Proverbs 16:3). Time spent planning and praying is very important.

4. A desire to learn. You will enjoy your studies more if you are able to:

- Open your mind and senses to new, perhaps conflicting, ideas and experiences.

- Read and write about and discuss questions that may or may not have answers.

- Look for principles and the basic unifying ideas in a subject.

- Establish links between new subject matter and your own practical experience of the world.

- Learn to study for a purpose. Be diligent to show thyself approved unto God (2 Timothy 2:15).

- Study for the purpose of renewing your mind toward God's purpose and will for your life (Romans 12:1-2, Ephesians 4:17ff.).

How to Read Better

A useful approach to studying is known as PQ4R, which stands for Preview, Question, Read, Reflect, Recite, Review (Thomas & Robinson, 1972). The process is as follows:

- *Preview* - introduce yourself to the material to obtain a general view of the course or assignment. This is done by using the skill called scanning. Scan the table of contents, the introduction, headings, emphasized sections, summaries, exercises, and final paragraphs.

• Think of *Questions* that are related to the purpose of your study and allow yourself to read with anticipation (e.g., "Why does the author divide up his material in this way?").

• *Read* the material. Read at a pace that is appropriate for the type of material being read. Light reading material can be read at a fast pace. Heavy theological discussion should be read carefully and at a pace that allows comprehension. Remember you are reading for comprehension and recall. Do so while paying attention to details which support your purposes. Also, learn to read prayerfully. (This is not part of the PQ4R method but is certainly a good idea!)

• Stop at the end of each section to reflect on what you read, and make notes regarding the main ideas and important details. Reflection is a very important step. It is during this time that you allow the ideas to "roam around" within your mind so that they connect with other ideas, facts, and life experiences. In so doing, you may have new ideas—a synthesis of material—which may help you grasp the inter-relatedness of all of God's creation or may help you find a new solution for an old problem. The stage of reflection is creative and is extremely valuable.

• After some reflection, go back to your questions and purposes. *Recite* these and attempt to connect them with your reflections in the previous step. This second attempt at making cognitive connections is a very important step, which will greatly facilitate long-term memory (recall). This is the step that seals the learning process and moves one from the memorization stage into learning, and thus the ability to recall at a later date is enhanced.

• *Review* what you have read (and test your notes for accuracy) by quickly reviewing the previous five steps.

During the Read Stage of PQ4R

• Look for the author's framework of ideas—the plan upon which he/she constructed the material. This is often revealed by the headings which may also indicate a flow.

• Pick out the main ideas in each paragraph, which are often contained in the first or last sentence.

• Do not ignore the author's diagrams and illustrations. They make things clear where the text may not.

• Think of your own examples. Look for applications in your own experience.

• Be critical. Do not take the author's work on trust. Look for him/her to justify statements he/she makes. (If he/she doesn't, and the point is an important one, check with another book or fellow student.)

• Work out what the results would be if theories other than the ones you are reading about were true.

• Do not be afraid to skip paragraphs and whole sections if you see that they are not relevant to your purpose. (There is no law that says that you must read every page of a book.)

• If, after reflecting for some time, you still find a section difficult to understand, take a break. Try to discuss the difficulty with other students, or find another author's treatment of the topic, and then come back and read it again, two or three times if necessary.

How to Make Useful Notes

It helps to make notes, as described earlier in this book. For the moment, consider the usefulness of note cards and notes.

• Note-taking will keep you active, and concentrating (so you learn and remember better).

• They provide a written record for review purposes.

• They protect you from the immense frustration that occurs when you recall a quotation or a source of information that fits precisely with what you have to say, but you cannot use it because you have not written it down.

APPENDIX B
Additional Sources of Help

These Internet sources may be useful in the process of doing research and writing a paper, thesis, or dissertation.

Tips on Writing Form and Style

APA Style.org
http://www.apastyle.org/

Advice on Research and Writing
http://www.cs.cmu.edu/afs/cs.cmu.edu/user/mleone/web/how-to.html

A Guide for Writing Research Papers
http://webster.commnet.edu/apa/apa_index.htm

Tips, Tools & Ideas to Improve Your Writing
http://www.aci-plus.com/tips/

So You Have to Do a Research Project?
http://www.ri.net/schools/East_Greenwich/research.html

Institute for Creation Research
This site has several different resources, including impact articles (monthly articles related to the creation/evolution controversy), research articles, books, radio programs, videos and cassettes.
http://www.icr.org

Leadership Journal
http://www.christianitytoday.com/leaders/

Theology Today Journal
http://theologytoday.ptsem.edu/

The Chalcedon Report
http://www.chalcedon.edu/report/issuesindex.shtml

KnightCite
Free citation maker on Calvin College website. Enter the data of a book or article into a template and it will put it into APA format. We find it cuter than helpful, and doubt that it is a timesaver, but try it out and if you find it helpful, use it.
http://webapps.calvin.edu/knightcite/

Free Research Sites and Journals

Alexandria Foundation
http://www.alexfound.org

Barna Research Group
http://www.barna.org

Christian Resources Institute
http://www.cresourcei.org

Christian Research Journal
http:// www.equip.org

Computer Assisted Theology
http://info.ox.ac.uk/ctitext/theology

Journal for Christian Theological Research
http://home.apu.edu/~CTRF/jctr.html

Educational Resources Information Center (ERIC) is a federally funded national information system that provides associated adjunct clearinghouses, and support components, a variety of services and products on a broad range of education related issues through its 16 subject-specific clearinghouses. "Ask ERIC" is a personalized Internet-based service providing education information to teachers, librarians, counselors, administrators, parents, and anyone interested in education throughout the United States and the world.
http://ericir.syr.edu/

Google Scholar – A relatively new site with items from sources that range from solid scholarly journals to popular press. Well worth visiting, but here—and everywhere—be sure you collect only factual material. If in doubt, throw it out.
http://scholar.google.com/

Internet Public Library - Ready Reference and index of 20,000+ books available full text on the Net
http://www.ipl.org/

Refdesk – This site bills itself as "The single best source for facts."
http://www.refdesk.com/

WorldCat – Website opens the catalogs of 10,000 libraries around the world to help you locate one of a billion books.

http://www.worldcat.org

Biography sites
http://www.biography.com
http://www.omnibiography.com/index.asp

Search Engines

Because Internet sites often move or disappear, you are encouraged to develop skills using the search engines.

Arts and Humanities
http://www.allsearchengines.com/arts.html

Indexes, Abstracts, Bibliographies, and Table of Contents Services
http://info.lib.uh.edu/indexes/indexes.htm

Pay Research Sites

These sites allow you to search for specific topics and then download and print articles.

Northern Lights
Very reasonably priced with a great guarantee. Allows a student to do research at home. The cost (usually $2.95/article) is well worth it compared to time, travel, and copy expenses incurred going to a library. http://www.northernlight.com/

Digital Dissertations
http://wwwlib.umi.com/dissertations/

Ask ERIC
Writing Research Papers: A Step-by-Step Procedure
http://owl.english.purdue.edu/handouts/research/_ressteps.html

Research Tools
http://www.acwpress.com/links.htm#research_tools

Using the Right Words
http://www.gospelcom.net/guide/resources/jargon.php

Christian Tips
http://christian.lifetips.com/PPF/id/56691/Cat.asp

Complete One Stop Resources

ICLnet   http://www.iclnet.org/
This site is extensive and contains a multitude of resources, including:

- Guide to Christian Missions on the Internet
  Organizations & Periodicals
- Guide to Christian Resources on the Internet
  Mail-Based Services
  Anonymous FTP Sites
  Christian College Web Sites
  Web Sites Directory
  Web Subjects Guide
  Periodicals
  Bulletin Board Systems
  USENET News Groups
- Guide to Christian Literature on the Internet
  Bibles
  Books
  Articles
  Sermons
  Bible Studies/Devotionals
  News Sources
  Newsletters/Periodicals
  Creeds/Confessions
  Publishers/Bookstores
- Guide to Early Church Documents on Internet
  Canonical Information
  Apostolic Fathers
  Patristic Texts
  Creeds and Canons
  Related Documents
- Reading Room
  The CFD E-Connection
  Creation Research Society
  Hedley Palmer Expositions
  IIis Company
  Institute of Practical Bible Education
  In Unison
  Jesus' Witnesses
  Nederlandse Bibliotheek
  New Life League
  Our Daily Break
  Project Wittenberg

ProLife News
Return to God
Sermon Notes on the Russian Gospel
Sion's Jewish Instruction Page
Sunday Snippets
Spurgeon's Sermons
Taize Community
United Reformed News Service
Voice of the Martyrs
David Wilkerson
- Software Library
- Directory of Christian Organizations
  Educational Institutions
  Organizations

Christian Apologetics and Research Ministry
http://www.carm.org/bible.htm
This is an extensive site with the following resources:
- The Bible
  The Bible Online
  Christian Doctrine
  Christian Issues
  Creeds and Confessions
  Devotions
  Dictionary of Theology
  Evangelism
  Misc. Information
  Parables
  Sermons
  Testimonies
  To the Christian Church
- Apologetics Info
  40 Objections
  Apologetics
  Apologetics Dialogues
  Christian Resources
  Heresies
  Lost Books

Research
- Questions
  About Doctrine
  About God
  About Jesus
  Other Questions
- Bible Difficulties
  Genesis – Deuteronomy
  Joshua – Esther
  Job - Song of Solomon
  Isaiah – Malachi
  Matthew – Mark
  Luke, John, & Acts
  Romans - Philemon
  Hebrews - Revelation
- Religious Movements
  About Cult Groups
  Religious Movements List
  Christadelphianism
  Christian Science
  Intern. Church of Christ
  Islam
  Jehovah's Witnesses
  Mormonism
  New Age Movement
  Oneness Pentecostal
  Roman Catholicism
  Seventh Day Adventism
  Shepherd's Chapel
  Universalism
- Secular Movements
  Abortion
  Atheism
  Creation-Evol. Debate
  Evolution
  Relativism
  Secular School
- More Stuff
  Audio

Discussion Boards
Features
More Stuff
Past Newsletters
What's New?

Christian Dictionary
http://www.carm.org/dictionary.htm

The following manuals are helpful:

Aaron, J. E. (2002). *The Little, Brown essential handbook for writers* (4th ed.). New York: Longman.

American Psychological Association. (2001). *Publication manual of the American Psychological Association* (5th ed.). Washington, DC: American Psychological Association.

Textbooks that may be helpful for understanding the procedures and methodologies of research:

Andrews, R. D. & Walters, R. P. (2008). *From questions to answers: Principles and methods of quantitative research.* (With tutorials on CD). Chattanooga, TN: High Ground Press. (Available from Vision Publishing.)

Ary, D., Jacobs, L. C., Razavieh, A., & Sorenson, C. K. (2007). *Introduction to research in education* (7th ed.). Belmont, CA: Wadsworth.

Gall, M. D., Gall., J. P. & Borg, W. R. (2006). *Educational research: An introduction* (8th ed.). Boston: Allyn & Bacon.

Mertler, C. A. & Charles, C. M. (2006). *Introduction to educational research* (6th ed.). Boston: Allyn & Bacon.

Tuckman, B. W., (1999). *Conducting educational research* (5th ed.). Fort Worth: Harcourt Brace College Publishers.

The Minister's Library [1]

These books are regarded as enduring classics, having gained long and widespread appreciation because they are practical and authoritative. Each of them has been in print by various publishers over the years. We suggest you consult used book vendors for copies.

Cruden, Alexander. *Cruden's complete concordance.*
Edersheim, Alfred. *The life and times of Jesus the Messiah.*
Hastings, James. *A dictionary of the Bible.*
Hastings, J. *A dictionary of the Bible.* Five Volumes.
Henry, M. *Matthew Henry's commentary on the whole Bible.* Six Volumes.
Lightfoot, J. *A commentary on the New Testament from the Talmud and Hebraica.* Four Volumes.
Matthews, V. H. *Manners and customs of the Bible.*
Nave, O. *Nave's topical Bible.*
Sheldon, H. C. *History of the Christian church.*
Vincent, M. R. *Vincent's word studies in the New Testament.* Four Volumes.
Wilson, W. *Wilson's Old Testament studies.*
Young, R. *Young's analytical concordance to the Bible.*

---

[1] The list is from: Bohac, J. J. & DeKoven, S. E. *An Introduction to Bible Study.* Ramona, CA: Vision Publishing.

For Students in Australasia

The pages that follow contain the standard guides that are issued to *VIU* students in Australia and New Zealand.

Writing a Thesis

Topic

Before starting your essay or thesis, a faculty member must approve the theme you have chosen. Consult with that person as early in the process as you can. The topic would normally be a biblical theme—an inquiry into some area of Christian living or doctrine that is related to a specific aspect of Christian service, ethics, or ministry, or to the structure, work, worship, history, or future of the church.

Presentation

You should type or print your essay, double spaced, on one side only of the paper. If you cannot type it yourself, arrange for someone else to do so. Include a title page containing your name, the title of the essay, and the date of its completion. Leave generous margins on all sides of your sheets, so that there is adequate room for the person who grades it to make appropriate comments. Make sure that each page is numbered, and staple or bind all the sheets together.

Structure

Your essay should be set up as follows:
- A title page, which should contain your name, address, the subject, and the date of completion.
- A table of contents, or outline, which should reflect as closely as possible the headings and subheadings used in the thesis
- Acknowledgments if appropriate (e.g., your typist or illustrator)
- A list of abbreviations (if any have been used)
- The body of the essay, broken up either into chapters, or sections, with appropriate headings and sub-headings
- Any appendices that may be needed
- A note on your methods of research

Documentation

A complete bibliography should be provided, listing the sources that you drew from and/or researched (see below, under "Research"). An addendum at the end of this document gives further information on how to set up footnotes, endnotes, and bibliographies.

Footnotes

You should include in your essay a system of footnotes and/or endnotes that identify sources of information used in the development of your work. Give the reference details in each note in the normal manner; that is, book title, author's name, publisher, place of publication, date, and page number. It is important that you clearly identify any part of the essay that does not strictly contain your own ideas or words. Direct quotes from another work must be set in quotation marks, with the source identified in a note. If you write a passage that substantially echoes another person's ideas or words, make sure to identify your source in a footnote or endnote. Plagiarism is not permissible within today's literary ethics.

Originality

The College does not expect you to be entirely original in your writing. You are free to draw from other materials (with proper acknowledgments). However, you should also introduce as much original research, thought, or experience, as you can. Give credit for the books or sources researched, the manner in which you have organized your material, the degree to which you have successfully analyzed and understood your material, and the extent of your creative or original thought or presentation.

Research

To gather materials you should use resources like the following:
- Published books
- Unpublished writings
- Interviews
- Journals and magazines
- Leaflets or brochures
- Government publications
- Audio and/or video tapes
- Your local library

• Computer research, the Internet, and the World-Wide-Web

Style

Write in a formal style, but avoid being too impersonal, abstract, or indirect. Give attention to correct spelling. Although this is not a course in English grammar, you can lose marks if your essay indicates carelessness or laziness. After all, spelling help is no farther away than a dictionary. If you find writing difficult, use short and simple sentences. Don't try to be more clever than you are. Get a more literate friend to check your work and offer suggestions for correcting faulty grammar or wrong spelling.

In all essays, the marker will be looking for some measure of original thought, and a good writing style. This is particularly true of essays or theses required for the higher awards. For example, we would expect a Masters thesis to show a substantial measure of creative analysis, and a better-than-average understanding of the subject.

Even more is that true of a doctoral thesis, which we would expect to display superior handling of the subject, and a high level of originality.

The use of direct quotations can add interest to your writing. A short passage—no more than three or four lines—can be included as part of the paragraph you are writing. Make sure you put it in quotation marks. However, a longer passage should be separated from your paragraph, and indented, as this one is. Since it would not be appropriate for another author's work to be graded or corrected, longer quotes can be typed in single-spacing. You will, of course, acknowledge the source of the quote either in a footnote or an endnote. If your resources allow it, the indented paragraph(s) can also be printed in a smaller type. Because the indentation marks the passage as a quote, there is no need (except for direct speech) to use quote marks.

Poetry should be centered, and set out as follows, taken from William Shakespeare's *Sonnet*. The poem could be set in italics, and single spaced.

> *Let me not to the marriage of true minds*
> *Admit impediments. Love is not love*
> *Which alters when it alteration finds,*
> *Or bends with the remover to remove.*

Oh, no! it is an ever-fixed mark
That looks on tempests, and is never shaken;
It is the star to every wand'ring bark,
Whose worth's unknown, although his height be taken.
Love's not Time's fool, though rosy lips and cheeks
Within his bending sickle's compass come;
Love alters not with his brief hours and weeks,
But bears it out even to the edge of doom.
If this be error and upon me prov'd,
I never writ, nor no man ever lov'd.

The same rules should be followed for Scripture citations. Short passages can be included in your paragraph; longer passages should be kept separate and indented. Biblical poetry should be laid out as poetry.

Method

Follow this procedure:

• Read all you can about your topic, taking notes as you read, and write an outline, or preliminary plan, of your essay.

• Gather primary materials (based on your own experience and thinking).

• Make sure that your notes contain a full record of each book, source, or interview from which you have drawn material.

• Use headings and subheadings, making sure that they follow each other in a logical order, and assist in the development of your argument and the clarity of your presentation.

• Write a first draft of your essay. Put the essay aside for two or three days; get someone else to review it for you.

• Revise and correct the first draft.

• If necessary, repeat the last step. Then type out the final draft, and type the number of words in your essay on the title page. (Don't count the words individually. Work out the average number of words on one page, and multiply that by the number of pages.)

• Send the completed essay to the College.

Footnotes and Bibliographies

Footnotes

Direct quotations from another work must always be marked by quotation marks in the body of your essay, and the source acknowledged in a footnote. A footnote may also be used to make an extra comment, or insert additional material that would be disruptive if it were placed in the body of the essay. In your text, you may indicate a footnote by a number, a letter, or some other mark.

For a work that has not previously been quoted in your essay, use the style shown in the footnote below for your footnotes or endnotes. Note the following:

- The author's name is given first (unless you have already given the full name in your text).
- The author's name is then followed by the name of the work (underlined).
- Publishing details are then recorded. Include all information: date, chapter title, page number. Note the use of commas and semicolons.

Here is an example: Jonathon Browne (editor), *Dictionary of World Religions*, article "Islamic Prayer;" Thompson & Thompson, London, 1987; pg. 335.

For a work that you have quoted before, use either *ibid.* or *op. cit.*
- *Ibid.* ("the same") is used when no other work has been quoted between this footnote and the one preceding it (even if several pages have intervened between the two quotations).

Here is an example: Ibid., pg. 398.
- *Op. cit.* ("the work cited") is used when one or more footnotes stand between the original quotation and the present one. The author's last name must be included, unless you have mentioned it in the text.

Here is an example: Anderson, Op. cit., pg. 35.

Bibliographies

Your essay/thesis must contain a bibliography listing all the sources to which you referred while you were preparing it. The bibliography should be the last item in your essay, and it should be set out as follows, showing where appropriate a book, article, author, editor, or compiler.

Blacker, G. J., *Dynamics of Grace*; Blonheim & Sons, New York, 1974; pg. 38.

Conrad, C. C., art. "Christ & Culture," *New Faith Journal*, April 1993; The Foundations Society, Glasgow; pg. 12.

Davids, G. H., et. al.; *Eight Scholars Speak*; J. J. Brown, London, 1976.

Ender, K. V., ed., *Songs of Love*; Lock & Co, London, 1991.

Preparing a Word Study

• Choose the word. For example, *reconciliation.*

• Use a word concordance to list the important occurrences in your Bible of *reconcile(d), reconciling,* or *reconciliation.*

• Use a topical concordance to list verses or passages which contain the idea of *reconciliation.*

• Look up the meaning of the word in: an English dictionary; Greek and/or Hebrew dictionaries; Greek and/or Hebrew word books; Bible dictionaries and/or encyclopedias. Write down these definitions and any other ideas or information that you find, or that come to your mind on the subject.

• Summarize the information you have gathered under four or five different headings. For example, what is reconciliation; how are we reconciled; with whom are we reconciled; when are we reconciled; what are the results of reconciliation, both now and in the future.

• Expand your summaries with your own comments, illustrations from scripture or life, and the like.

• Write a final version of your study.

Note that many study Bibles contain examples of word studies that you could use as a guide. Also, the word studies in your lecture notes will show how to outline and present your study.

Writing an Essay

This section deals with writing a small essay of around two thousand words. For longer documents, see Section I above on "Writing a Thesis."

Presentation

Your essay should be typed, if possible. If not, then it must be written neatly in ink. Essays that are illegible or unreasonably difficult to read will be returned unmarked. Include a title page, containing your name, the title of the essay, and the date of its completion. Make sure that each page is correctly numbered, and staple or bind the sheets together.

Research

Even for a short essay you should try to do some research beyond your primary textbook, including the study of sources that give a contrary view.

Structure

Your essay should have a clear beginning, followed by the body of your argument, and then the conclusion.

Documentation

A bibliography should be added, listing all your sources of information. Place this at the end of your essay.

Originality

We do not expect your work to be entirely original. You are free to draw from other materials (with proper acknowledgment). However, you should include as much original thought or experience as you can. But remember that an essay is not a personal testimony or biography. Use anecdotes about your own life, or about other people, sparingly.

Style

Write in a generally formal style, avoiding slang, or colloquial expressions; but don't be too impersonal, abstract, or indirect. Use active sentences as much as possible, not passive. For example, the paragraph just above could have been expressed passively thus: "It is not expected that your work will be entirely original." It reads livelier when it is cast actively: "We do not expect . . ." But sometimes a passive structure is less obtrusive, as in the first part of the previous two sentences.

Method

Follow this procedure. Some of these things may not be applicable to you now, but will be good to know as you progress to higher levels:
- Read all you can about your topic, taking notes as you read, and jot down an outline or preliminary plan of your essay.
- Gather primary ideas, based on your own experience and thought.
- Make sure that your notes contain full details of each book, source, or interview from which you have drawn material.
- If your essay contains quotes from, or passages that closely echo other writings, make sure to note this in footnotes and/or endnotes (see your textbooks for examples of how this should be done).
- Organize your notes to match your outline (you may find it useful to put each group of notes on separate sheets of paper).
- Write a first draft of your essay.
- Put it aside for two or three days.
- Get someone else to review it for you.
- Revise and correct your first draft.
- If necessary, repeat the previous three steps, once, twice, or three times.
- Type out or print the final version.
- Type the number of words in your essay on the title page (don't count the words individually; work out the average number of words on one page, and multiply that by the number of pages).
- Send the completed essay to the appropriate office.

Study Guidelines

Here are some guidelines that will help you to get the best possible enjoyment and benefit out of studying your textbooks and doing the assignments.

Developing Good Practice

- Give a high priority to the program until you have obtained the award you desire, which means (a) you should write the class times into your calendar and keep those times free from other commitments; and (b) you should be prepared to sacrifice other activities and entertainments for the duration of the course.
- Accept the discipline of reading right through your textbook within the month allowed, and of completing your exam before the next subject begins. If you fall behind in your studies you will find it difficult to catch up, and it may lead you to abandon the program. Those who start do not please God, but those who finish!
- Begin each study period with a simple and brief prayer, yet one that recognizes that only the presence and illumination of the Holy Spirit can turn your study time into a supernatural event. Study with an expectation both that your mind will be instructed and that the Word of God will transform your life. Expect to hear from God! If His voice is not mingled with what you read, then you read in vain.
- Set apart a period of time each week when you will be able to make study your top priority. Choose a time when you will have the fewest interruptions, away from other activities and family traffic. Try to keep to the same time each day or each week, so that you develop regular habits of study, perhaps while you commute to work. For example, one of our students modified a briefcase into a kind of study desk, complete with a small lamp and writing platform, so that he could study while he was a passenger in a car. Bus time and train time can be used in the same way.
- Turn off the radio and television, so that you can have the quietness you will need to meditate on and to pray about the things you are reading. Find, if you can, a reasonably quiet and private spot. At the least, you should try to set up a corner somewhere that you can use consistently as a place of study. Developing a familiar environment, as free as possible from distractions, is a great help

to concentration. Use a desk or table without clutter, and a comfortable chair. Avoid lounge chairs. The attitude of the body helps to determine the attitude of the mind. A lethargic body tends toward a slumbering mind.

- Let your family know that you are studying so that they will avoid interrupting you. If phone calls come, arrange for a message to be taken, or to return the call later.

Handling Your Textbook

- Scan through your textbook, to get a general sense of its contents and layout, and how its ideas are developed. Then choose the particular section you are planning to study, and read through it quickly, without pausing to look up Bible references or to take notes (unless an important idea occurs to you).
- Next, read the same section again, carefully, looking up all the references, making your own notes, working on difficult points until you understand them, making your own outline of the section, and re-writing the key ideas in your own words.
- Make sure you understand what you are reading. If something is not clear, ask the Lord to give you understanding. If you come across unfamiliar words in your textbook, look them up in a dictionary. Read the scripture verses mentioned in your textbook. Use a modern translation of the Bible. It is a good idea to have several different translations on hand, all of which you should aim to read at least once from cover to cover.
- Close your book and meditate on what you have read. Try to recall the main ideas and the sequence in which they were developed. Build the arguments again in your own mind. Join prayer with your meditation, for this is the time when the things you are studying can become a revelation of God in your spirit.
- Open the book again, and answer the questions on your exam paper that relate to the section you have just studied. Remember, the exams are all "open book." Indeed, you will not be able to answer many of the questions unless you do refer to your textbook. So, make full use of the book as you answer each question. You are not expected to work from memory alone.
- You can probably pass the exam without doing all the above. But surely, you have a higher goal than merely achieving a passing grade. If your larger purpose is the glory of God and your personal

enrichment, then don't forget that you will get out of your study only what you put into it.

- We have striven to achieve two things in the textbooks you will use: a high level of spiritual revelation; and (in most of them) a high literary quality. Therefore, you may find it useful to have at hand a good English dictionary, along with a Bible Encyclopedia or Bible Dictionary.

- And of course you will have a program for reading your Bible right through, repeatedly, for the rest of your life. There is not much point in going to Bible School if the only book you don't read is the Bible!

Samuel Johnson

In a letter to his friend James Boswell, dated December 8, 1763, the great lexicographer Samuel Johnson wrote:

(There once was a young man who) hoped that he should appear to attain, amidst all the ease of carelessness, and all the tumult of diversion, that knowledge and those accomplishments which mortals of the common fabric obtain only by mute abstraction and solitary drudgery. He tried this scheme of life awhile, was made weary of it by his sense and his virtue; he then wished to return to his studies; and finding long habits of idleness and pleasure harder to be cured than he expected . . . resolved the common consequences of irregularity into an unalterable decree of destiny, and concluded that Nature had originally formed him incapable of rational employment.[2]

Let all such fancies, illusive and destructive, be banished henceforward from your thoughts forever. Resolve, and keep your resolution; choose, and pursue your choice. If you spend this day in study, you will find yourself still more able to study tomorrow; not that you are to expect that you shall at once obtain a complete victory. Depravity is not very easily overcome. Resolution will sometimes relax, and diligence will sometimes be interrupted; but let no accidental surprise or deviation, whether short or long, dispose you to despondency. Consider these failings as incident to all mankind. Begin again where you left off, and endeavor to avoid the seducements that prevailed over you before.

---

[2] Over the years I have myself met many like that young man, who blame God, or Providence or parents for their supposed inability to study hard and therefore hold themselves blameless for failing to advance in knowledge and maturity.

This, my dear Boswell, is advice which, perhaps, has been often given you, and given you without effect. But this advice, if you will not take from others, you must take from your own reflections, if you purpose to do the duties of the station to which the bounty of Providence has called you.[3]

---

[3] James Boswell, *Life of Johnson, Aetat. 54; Thursday, December 8, 1763.*

About the CD

The CD that comes with this book has two types of helpful material:

1. Three PowerPoint presentations that will play on any PC-style computer. If the computer does not have Microsoft PowerPoint on it, a PowerPoint player can be downloaded from the CD.

Ordinarily the CD will load up automatically. It will play better on many computers if the files are first downloaded onto the hard drive. You may view the presentation at your own pace simply by clicking to advance to the next slide when you are ready. There is no soundtrack.

Form And Style is in two parts. The first part is a short tutorial about two issues in writing style: *person* and *tense*. The second part is a series of slides that alternate from a question to its answer on the next slide (or several slides). The other two PowerPoint shows are in this format. On your first viewing, go through without pressure to learn everything. It takes time to master the "ins and outs" of good writing. You can come back any time to review and learn more.

2. Files 4 through 6 are prototype pages in Microsoft Word. The Title Page is used at both undergraduate and graduate levels. The Certification page is usually required only for a thesis, dissertation, or doctoral project. Adapt the wording to suit your project.

Index to Tracks on the CD
1. *Form And Style* PPt file
2. *Hypotheses And Definitions* PPt file
3. *Logic And Content* PPt file
4. Title Page MSWord file
5. Certification Page MSWord file
6. Table of Contents MSWord file

About The Authors

Dr. Rich Walters is Dean of Pastoral Care and Counseling, Vision International University. This follows an active career as a licensed psychologist. The author of 18 books, and many articles and training manuals, he has supervised research at undergraduate, master's, and doctoral levels. His Ph.D. in Counseling Psychology is from the University of Georgia. The father of a son and daughter, he lives with his wife in Chattanooga, TN.

Dr. Stan DeKoven is the founder and President of Vision International Educational Network, headquartered in Ramona, CA, but active in 145 countries. He is the author of more than 35 books on practical Christian ministry, leadership, and counseling. Dr. DeKoven is a graduate of San Diego State University, Webster University, and the Professional School of Psychological Studies, where he completed his Ph.D. in Counseling Psychology. He is the father of two daughters, has three grandchildren, and resides in Ramona, CA.